HAMILTONIAN PRINCIPLES

Hamiltonian Principles

Extracts from the writings of Alexander Hamilton

James Truslow Adams

Simon Publications

2001

Originally published by Little, Brown, and Company

Library of Congress Control Number: 28007627

ISBN: 1-931541-48-5

Printed by Lightning Source Inc. La Vergne, TN

Published by Simon Publications, P. O. Box 321, Safety Harbor, FL 34695

INTRODUCTION

IT is fitting that a volume of extracts from the works of Hamilton should be published as a companion to the similar one displaying the principles of Jefferson. The bitter personal contest between the two men belongs to the history of the past, but the contest between their contrasted systems of thought belongs to the living present.

As in the case of Jefferson, no attempt will be made in this Introduction to narrate, even briefly, the biographical details of Hamilton's life. They can be found ably, if not always impartially, told in many volumes. Nor is it needful here to elaborate a comparison between the two leaders or their schools of thought. Such a comparison may be readily drawn by the reader himself from the extracts selected.

In both volumes the editor has tried to choose such passages as are of general application and abiding interest rather than such as might elucidate or justify actions or episodes in the lives of the writers. Both volumes are intended to be not footnotes to history or biography, but handy compendiums of the body of principles developed by their authors. Anyone familiar with the writings of Hamilton will realize that this plan is more difficult of execution in his case than in Jefferson's. All of Hamilton's writings are remarkably cogent, closely reasoned, logical, and clear, but they are also diffuse. He had the lawyer's love of piling phrase on phrase and letting no possible shade of meaning escape.

He was not a philosopher, nor was he in any great degree an original thinker. He did not have an inquiring mind, and the range of his interests was comparatively narrow. I have never, for example, come across a word by him on education nor does the heading appear in the index to his collected works. On the other hand, in the practical application of his political faith to the problems confronting the new country, no one surpassed him, and no man of his time left a deeper impress upon the form of the nation than he. Nor did any of the Fathers leave a more influential body of expressed doctrine than did he in his papers comprised in the *Federalist*.

Hamilton's fundamental idea, which it is needful to emphasize in order to understand the political edifice which he tried to erect, was distrust of the common man. He believed that the great generality of men were incapable of self-government, due to ignorance, selfishness, absence of self-control and other qualities — or lack of them. Looking back over history, he rightly saw that this had always been the case. Looking ahead, he saw no reason to believe it would ever be any different. Human nature, he thought, would not change. Thoroughly convinced of that, and being a practical man without the dreams of an enthusiast or idealist, the inferences he drew were obvious.

He did not limit his distrust to the common people. He distrusted human nature itself and believed that the spring of action which could most safely be counted upon was self-interest. He was himself a self-made man and had much of the self-made man's admiration for success and contempt for failure, as he himself judges both. A poor immigrant, with the shadow of the bar sinister cast across his path, he had nevertheless achieved a distinguished position, married the daughter of a financially and socially prominent family, and, through his own energy and ability, become one of the leaders of the country at an age when most men were beginning their careers. His acquaintance with men

INTRODUCTION

in various ranks of society had led him to the belief that all ranks had their peculiar virtues and vices, but that the vices of the rich would be less dangerous for a governing class than would the vices of the poor. All these facts must be taken into consideration in tracing the roots of his political philosophy.

On such a basis Hamilton proceeded to develop his ideas. Talk about liberty in the abstract did not greatly interest him. He was too practical and it appeared foolish to prate much about liberty when it seemed too unfortunately evident that men in the mass were not capable of governing themselves. In a democracy he could foresee only eventual anarchy, with liberty for no one. He recognized the necessity of going further toward a republican form of government than he would have liked, because the people at large had come to expect so much that something had to be given to them, but as to the real organs of government, he thought they should be kept as far as possible in the hands of those who by their position in society showed that they had ability to govern and property interests to protect. It is obvious why Hamilton was not interested in the idea of popular education and of gradually lifting the entire mass of possible electors to a position where they might be more capable of self-government. Owing to his distrust of human nature, that plan would appear to him to have nothing practical in it. He may have been right. The problem is by no means solved after two centuries of red schoolhouses and mass production in universities. This Introduction is not intended as a critique, but an outline of Hamilton's political philosophy. That philosophy he had a unique opportunity to impress upon the country, as a member of the Constitutional Convention which drafted the Constitution, as the leading advocate for its adoption, and as the chief cabinet officer in the first years of establishing the new government.

It was clear what he would try to do in putting his general concepts into practice. In the first place, both the scheme of government and its practical operation must be so devised as to keep the common people as much out of it as was possible, compatible with their pretensions to power. As far as might be, the reins must be in the hands of the successful, to ensure ability and stability both. If the people were not capable of governing, they must be governed.

INTRODUCTION

To do that implied concentrated strength in the central government. Instead of keeping the power as near the people as could be, in a gradation of lessened duties upward from town meetings to Federal Congress, letting each do all possible before transmitting powers and duties to the one above, Hamilton reversed the structure, and desired that the Federal government should be the main source of power. In the conflict between the nation and the states, it was the states he feared as the future destroyers of liberty, because he felt that the only liberty for the people themselves which could be achieved would be that permitted to the individual by the strength of the governors, not a doctrinaire liberty which inhered by any natural process in the governed themselves.

Almost the entire body of Hamilton's writing is devoted, directly or indirectly, to the problem of strengthening the central, that is the Federal, organ of government. But there was one other fundamental idea at the bottom of all his plans. There would be no use in having a government strong in powers on paper unless it could exert that power in practice. Hamilton recognized that the world had gone too far to rely solely on force, although he never hesitated to invoke it. He realized that in some way a favorable public opinion would have to be organized. A government of the many by the few could not exist without it. The strongest element in human nature would have to be enlisted on its behalf. That element he believed to be self-interest, and self-interest to be manifested most strongly in money matters. From the start, therefore, he undertook to push through measures which would not only enlist the moneyed interest of the new country on the side of government but would enlarge both the extent and numbers of such interest. His part as statesman would be to tie up the success of all who had money with the success of the government, to tie them so closely as to make the success of the government an inevitable element in their personal successes. To do that with such moneyed men as already existed, would be the first step. To increase the number of moneyed men, would be the second. An independent farmer might be a rebellious subject. A man who had money in government bonds or whose business was dependent upon a tariff made by the government, would be a loyal citizen. If this idea, in the stark simplicity of its psychology and logic, seems somehow rather remote from the Declaration of Independence, it must be admitted, nevertheless, to have been enormously successful in practice then and ever since.

Most of the extracts which follow will be found to be variations on these few simple themes. They cover, to a great extent, the same ground traversed in the extracts in the first section of the Jefferson volume. The reader may compare them, topic for topic. It may be noted that, owing to the nature of Hamilton's state papers, the extracts do not do full justice to the superb logical development of his ideas. For that reason some further comment on his practical application of them may be permissible and useful.

The selections on "The People," as well as references scattered elsewhere, show clearly his attitude in that regard, though none of them is as forcibly expressed as his remark in conversation: "Your People, Sir, your People is a great beast." His desire for a strong central government is brought out in many of the extracts, and not only in those which are more particularly grouped under that topic. It was in his writings especially on the formation of a government bank that Hamilton developed his ideas on the powers of the Federal government to their greatest extent. It was for the express purpose of making possible the establishment of that institution, which was to be the keystone of his entire financial system, that he found it necessary to proclaim his theory of *implied* powers. It has been, of course, this theory, now almost universally accepted, which has permitted and fostered the colossal and originally unintended growth of the national as contrasted with the state governments. What Jefferson feared and what Hamilton scarce dared hope, has come to pass, and, in spite of much talk about "sovereignty," the states have become for most purposes merely administrative units. It may be noted that in this respect the trends in the two great English-speaking empires have been opposite for a century and more. Whereas the larger units of the British Empire are steadily becoming more independent and self-governing, in the United States they have as steadily lost their independent life and been absorbed into the larger power of the Union.

If in his papers on the Bank Hamilton laid the foundations for the colossal extension of Federal powers, it was in his "Report on the

INTRODUCTION

National Credit " that he brought the money power and the nation into close alliance. It is one of his longest and most important state papers, but singularly unquotable in bits. His plan was to enlist the support for government of all those who had money to invest by funding the state and national debts. A large part of these were in the hands of merchants, financiers, and gamblers, all of whom would at once become staunch defenders of the social order as soon as the much depreciated securities were made to be worth par by the act of assumption. Perhaps no other scheme of Hamilton's created more bitter opposition on the part of those who were among the "have-nots," but it was immediately and immensely successful in enlisting the support of all the richer classes.

But Hamilton was aware that a wider base than such as was thus provided would become necessary. Numbers as well as riches were needed in increasing measure on the side of government. He placed little or no confidence in the self-governing ability of the small farmer, and ninety per cent of the population was then agricultural. Even of the class of rich men, only a portion could be directly linked to the chariot of government by owning a share in it.

INTRODUCTION

It was, for the most part, only the city men who had idle cash, whereas most of the large landed proprietors were apt to be borrowers rather than lenders. It was evidently necessary to create a new class of moneyed men, for the number of merchants would always bear a more or less fixed proportion to the number of farmers. This accounts for the extraordinarily able " Report on Manufactures." By building up manufactures on a large scale, to replace to a great extent the old household industries, Hamilton saw that he could make two strokes at once. He could not only bring into being great numbers of wealthy men with liquid property instead of land, but, by means of a favorable tariff, he could make them directly dependent upon government; and he believed that they would thus become even stauncher supporters perhaps than the bondholders. Moreover, there was the possibility that bondholders might be paid off in time, a fear which is expressed by him in his earnest pleas for a "national debt" as a "national blessing." Another moneyed group, strongly supporting law and order, would have to be built up to take their places. The plan succeeded as he intended and has developed beyond his wildest dreams.

INTRODUCTION

There is little evidence that Hamilton was stirred by the liberal movement of thought which was well under way even in his time. He matured young. By twenty-five he had acquired apparently most if not all of the general ideas he ever possessed. From then on he devoted himself with extraordinary ability to working them out in practice. His terms of thought were national wealth, power, law, order, stability. He concentrated on these, but rarely thought in terms of the improvement and happiness of the individual citizens of all ranks. He did not have the vision, which so possessed Jefferson, of a possible new order in which the common man might be happier, wiser, and better than he had been. Indeed, Jefferson himself feared that his dream might fade if America became, according to the standards of even that day, industrial, crowded, city-built, as was Europe.

Hamilton was a realist. As one reads volume after volume of his works, one feels an increasing admiration for the directness and force with which he hammers and moulds the glowing metal of the new nation to his own shape, but one also senses a hardness in the man, a lack of subtlety and of generous imagination. It may

[xvi]

be that without a vision men shall die. It is no less true that, without hard practical sense, they shall also die. Without Jefferson the new nation might have lost its soul. Without Hamilton it would assuredly have been killed in body. The Americans had never been able to govern themselves in larger units than parishes or towns or, at the most, individual colonies. In every single instance in which they had attempted concerted action, the meanness, the jealousy, the parsimoniousness of their narrowly provincial minds had wrecked the attempt. In the condition of the Congress there was every indication that such would again be the case and that the new United States would once more dissolve into thirteen feeble, independent states, quarreling among themselves and helpless before a foreign foe. I think it not too much to say that such would have unquestionably been the case had it not been for Hamilton. His one idea was to build a strong Ship of State and see to it that it was well defended with the most powerful guns he could place aboard. Jefferson was thinking in terms of the welfare of the crew. We needed both men then. We need the elements of thought which each yet contributes to American life to-day, but in order to have a unified national consciousness, a national soul with a single purpose, we have got to compose their apparently conflicting philosophies into a more harmonious whole than the toil of subduing a continent, the clashes of class interests, and the lack of sustained thought, have yet allowed us to consummate.

CHRONOLOGY

CONTENTS

ON GOVERNMENT

NOTE

The selections are made from *The Works of Alexander Hamilton*, edited by the late Henry Cabot Lodge, and published by G. P. Putnam's Sons, 1885. The volume and page references at the end of each extract refer to that edition.

ON GOVERNMENT

OBJECTS OF GOVERNMENT

THERE are two objects in forming systems of government — safety for the people, and energy in the administration. When these objects are united, the certain tendency of the system will be to the public welfare. If the latter object be neglected, the people's security will be as certainly sacrificed as by disregarding the former. Good constitutions are formed upon a comparison of the liberty of the individual with the strength of government. If the tone of either be too high, the other will be weakened too much. It is the happiest possible mode of conciliating these objects, to institute one branch peculiarly endowed with sensibility, another with knowledge and firmness. Through the opposition and mutual control of these bodies, the government will reach, in its operations, the perfect balance between liberty and power. — *Speech on the Senate of the United States*, June 25, 1788. Vol. I, p. 459.

HAMILTONIAN PRINCIPLES

A good government implies two things: first, fidelity to the object of government, which is the happiness of the people; secondly, a knowledge of the means by which that object can be best attained. Some governments are deficient in both these qualities; most governments are deficient in the first. I scruple not to assert, that in American governments too little attention has been paid to the last. The federal constitution avoids this error; and what merits particular notice, it provides for the last in a mode which increases the security of the first. — *The Federalist.* Vol. IX, p. 388.

The True Principle of Government

The true principle of government is this — make the system complete in its structure; give a perfect proportion and balance to its parts, and the powers you give it will never affect your security. The question, then, of the division of powers between the General and State governments, is a question of convenience. It becomes a prudential inquiry, what powers are proper to be reserved to the latter, and this immediately involves another inquiry into the proper objects of the two governments. This is the criterion by which we shall determine the just distribution of powers.

The great leading objects of the Federal Government, in which revenue is concerned, are to maintain domestic peace, and provide for the common defence. In these are comprehended the regulation of commerce — that is, the whole system of foreign intercourse, the support of armies and navies, and of the civil administration. It is useless to go into detail. Every one knows that the objects of the General Government are numerous, extensive, and important. Every one must acknowledge the necessity of giving powers, in all respects, and in every degree, equal to these objects. This principle assented to, let us inquire what are the objects of the State governments. Have they to provide against foreign invasion? Have they to maintain fleets and armies? Have they any concern in the regulation of commerce, the procuring alliances, or forming treaties of peace? No. Their objects are merely civil and domestic, to support the legislative establishment, and to provide for the administration of the laws. — *Speech on the Senate of the United States*, June 27, 1788. Vol. I, pp. 470–471.

HAMILTONIAN PRINCIPLES

Justice the End of Government

Justice is the end of government. It is the end of civil society. It ever has been and ever will be pursued until it be obtained, or until liberty be lost in the pursuit. In a society under the forms of which the stronger faction can readily unite and oppress the weaker, anarchy may as truly be said to reign as in a state of nature, where the weaker individual is not secured against the violence of the stronger; and as, in the latter state, even the stronger individuals are prompted, by the uncertainty of their condition, to submit to a government which may protect the weak as well as themselves; so, in the former state, will the more powerful factions or parties be gradually induced, by a like motive, to wish for a government which will protect all parties, the weaker as well as the more powerful. It can be little doubted that if the State of Rhode Island was separated from the Confederacy and left to itself, the insecurity of rights under the popular form of government within such narrow limits would be displayed by such reiterated oppression of factious majorities that some power altogether independent of the people would soon be called for by the voice of the very factions whose misrule had proved the necessity of it. In the extended republic of the United States, and among the great variety of interests, parties, and sects which it embraces, a coalition of a majority of the whole society could seldom take place on any other principles than those of justice and the general good; whilst there being thus less danger to a minor from the will of a major party, there must be less pretext, also, to provide for the security of the former, by introducing into the government a will not dependent on the latter, or, in other words, a will independent of the society itself. It is no less certain than it is important, notwithstanding the contrary opinions which have been entertained, that the larger the society, provided it lie within a practical sphere, the more duly capable it will be of self-government. And happily for the *republican cause*, the practicable sphere may be carried to a very great extent, by a judicious modification and mixture of the *federal principle. — The Federalist*. Vol. IX, pp. 326–327.

INHERENT STRENGTH OF GOOD GOVERNMENT

I will venture to assert that no combination of designing men under heaven will be capable of making a government unpopular which is in its principles a wise and good one, and vigorous in its operations. — *Speech on the Constitution,* June 21, 1788. Vol. I, p. 437.

THE TRUE PRINCIPLE OF A REPUBLIC

After all, we must submit to this idea, that the true principle of a republic is that the people should choose whom they please to govern them. Representation is imperfect in proportion as the current of popular favor is checked. This great source of free government, popular election, should be perfectly pure, and the most unbounded liberty allowed. Where this principle is adhered to; where, in the organization of the government, the legislative, executive, and judicial branches are rendered distinct; where, again, the legislative is divided into separate houses, and the operations of each are controlled by various checks and balances, and above all by the vigilance and weight of the State governments, to talk of tyranny and the subversion of our liberties, is to speak the language of enthusiasm. This balance between the National and State governments ought to be dwelt on with peculiar attention, as it is of the utmost importance. It forms a double security to the people. If one encroaches on their rights they will find a powerful protection in the other. Indeed, they will both be prevented from overpassing their constitutional limits by a certain rivalship, which will ever subsist between them. I am persuaded that firm union is as necessary to perpetuate our liberties as it is to make us respectable; and experience will probably prove that the National Government will be as natural a guardian of our freedom as the State Legislatures themselves. — *Speech on the Compromises of the Constitution*, June 21, 1788. Vol. I, pp. 436–437.

Civil Liberty

Natural liberty is a gift of the beneficent Creator to the whole human race, and . . . civil liberty is founded in that, and cannot be wrested from any people without the most manifest violation of justice. *Civil liberty is only natural liberty, modified and secured by the sanctions of civil society.* It is not a thing, in its own nature, precarious and dependent on human will and caprice, but it is conformable to the constitution of man, as well as necessary to the *well-being* of society. — *The Farmer Refuted*, 1775. Vol. I, p. 83.

HAMILTONIAN PRINCIPLES

Arbitrary Government

You are mistaken when you confine arbitrary government to a monarchy. It is not the supreme power being placed in one, instead of many, that discriminates an arbitrary from a free government. When any people are ruled by laws, in framing which they have no part, that are to bind them, to all intents and purposes, without, in the same manner, binding the legislators themselves, they are, in the strictest sense, slaves; and the government, with respect to them, is despotic. Great Britain is itself a free country, but it is only so because its inhabitants have a share in the legislature. — *The Farmer Refuted*, 1775. Vol. I, p. 77.

Freedom and Slavery

The only distinction between freedom and slavery consists in this: In the former state a man is governed by the laws to which he has given his consent, either in person or by his representative; in the latter, he is governed by the will of another. In the one case, his life and property are his own; in the other they depend upon the pleasure of his master. It is easy to discern which of these two states is preferable. No man in his senses can hesitate in choosing to be free, rather than a slave.

That Americans are entitled to freedom is incontestable on every rational principle. All men have one common original: they participate in one common nature, and consequently they have one common right. No reason can be assigned why one man should exercise any power or preeminence over his fellow-creatures more than another; unless they have voluntarily vested him with it. Since, then, Americans have not, by any act of theirs, empowered the British Parliament to make laws for them, it follows they can have no just authority to do it. — *A Full Vindication*, 1774. Vol. I, pp. 5–6.

FACTIONS

Much has been said about factions. As far as my observation has extended, factions in Congress have arisen from attachment to State prejudices. We are attempting by this Constitution to abolish factions, and to unite all parties for the general welfare. That a man should have the power, in private life, of recalling his agent, is proper; because, in the business in which he is engaged, he has no other object but to gain the approbation of his principal. Is this the case with the Senator ? Is he simply the agent of the State ? No. He is an agent for the Union, and he is bound to perform services necessary to the good of the whole, though his State should condemn them. Sir, in contending for a rotation, the gentlemen carry their zeal beyond all reasonable bounds. — *Speech on the Senate of the United States*, June 25, 1788. Vol. I, pp. 464–465.

Responsibility in Government

Why has government been instituted at all ? Because the pasions of men will not conform to the dictates of reason and justice, without constraint. Has it been found that bodies of men act with more rectitude or greater disinterestedness than individuals ? The contrary of this has been inferred by all accurate observers of the conduct of mankind; and the inference is founded upon obvious reasons. Regard to reputation has a less active influence, when the infamy of a bad action is to be divided among a number, than when it is to fall singly upon one. A spirit of faction, which is apt to mingle its poison in the deliberations of all bodies of men, will often hurry the persons of whom they are composed into improprieties and excesses, for which they would blush in a private capacity. — *The Federalist.* Vol. IX, p. 89.

OBEDIENCE TO LAW

If it were to be asked, What is the most sacred duty, and the greatest source of security in a republic? the answer would be, An inviolable respect for the Constitution and laws — the first growing out of the last. It is by this, in a great degree, that the rich and the powerful are to be restrained from enterprises against the common liberty — operated upon by the influence of a general sentiment, by their interest in the principle, and by the obstacles which the habit it produces erects against innovation and encroachment. It is by this, in a still greater degree, that caballers, intriguers, and demagogues are prevented from climbing on the shoulders of faction to the tempting seats of usurpation and tyranny. . . .

Government is frequently and aptly classed under two descriptions — a government of *force*, and a government of *laws;* the first is the definition of despotism — the last, of liberty. But how can a government of laws exist when the laws are disrespected and disobeyed?

HAMILTONIAN PRINCIPLES

Government supposes control. It is that *power* by which individuals in society are kept from doing injury to each other, and are brought to cooperate to a common end. The instruments by which it must act are either the *authority* of the laws or *force*. If the first be destroyed, the last must be substituted; and when this becomes the ordinary instrument of government, there is an end to liberty!

Those, therefore, who preach doctrines, or set examples which undermine or subvert the authority of the laws, lead us from freedom to slavery; they incapacitate us for a *government* of *laws*, and consequently prepare the way for one of *force*, for mankind must have *government of one sort or another*. There are, indeed, great and urgent cases where the bonds of the Constitution are manifestly transgressed, or its constitutional authorities so exercised as to produce unequivocal oppression on the community, and to render resistance justifiable. But such cases can give no color to the resistance by a comparatively inconsiderable part of a community, of constitutional laws distinguished by no extraordinary features of rigor or oppression, and acquiesced in by the body of the community. — *"Tully,"* 1794. Vol. VI, pp. 26–27.

HAMILTONIAN PRINCIPLES

Laws

The internal effects of a mutable policy are still more calamitous. It poisons the blessing of liberty itself. It will be of little avail to the people, that the laws are made by men of their own choice, if the laws be so voluminous that they cannot be read, or so incoherent that they cannot be understood; if they be repealed or revised before they are promulgated, or undergo such incessant changes that no man, who knows what the law is today, can guess what it will be tomorrow. Law is defined to be a rule of action; but how can that be a rule, which is little known, and less fixed? — *The Federalist*. Vol. IX, p. 390.

The Sanctions of Law

Government implies the power of making laws. It is essential to the idea of a law, that it be attended with a sanction; or, in other words, a penalty or punishment for disobedience. If there be no penalty annexed to disobedience, the resolutions or commands which pretend to be laws will, in fact, amount to nothing more than advice or recommendation. This penalty, whatever it may be, can only be

inflicted in two ways : by the agency of the courts
and ministers of justice, or by military force;
by the *coercion* of the magistracy, or by the
coercion of arms. The first kind can evidently
apply only to men ; the last kind must of necessity, be employed against bodies politic, or
communities, or States. It is evident that
there is no process of a court by which the
observance of the laws can, in the last resort,
be enforced. Sentences may be denounced
against them for violations of their duty; but
these sentences can only be carried into execution by the sword. In an association where the
general authority is confined to the collective
bodies of the communities that compose it,
every breach of the laws must involve a state
of war; and military execution must become
the only instrument of civil obedience. Such a
state of things can certainly not deserve the
name of government, nor would any prudent
man choose to commit his happiness to it. —
The Federalist. Vol. IX, p. 88.

Revenue Laws and Public Morality

The Secretary . . . begs leave to remark,
that there appear to him two leading principles,
one or the other of which must necessarily char-

acterize whatever plan [for revenue] may be adopted. One of them makes the *security* of the *revenue* to depend chiefly on the *vigilance* of the *public officers;* the other rests it essentially on the *integrity* of the *individuals* interested to avoid the payment of it.

The first is the basis of the plan submitted by the Secretary; the last has pervaded most if not all the systems which have hitherto been practised upon in different parts of the United States. The oaths of the dealers have been almost the only security for their compliance with the laws.

It cannot be too much lamented that these have been found an inadequate dependence. But experience has, on every trial, manifested them to be such. Taxes or duties relying for their collection on that security wholly, or almost wholly, are uniformly unproductive. And they cannot fail to be unequal, as long as men continue to be discriminated by unequal portions of rectitude. The most conscientious will pay most; the least conscientious least.

The impulse of interest, always sufficiently strong, acts with peculiar force in matters of this kind, in respect to which a loose mode of thinking is too apt to prevail. The want of a

habit of appreciating properly the nature of
the public rights renders that impulse in such
cases too frequently an overmatch for the sense
of obligation, and the evasions which are perceived, or suspected to be practised by some,
prompt others to imitation, by the powerful
motive of self-defence. They infer that they
must follow the example, or be unable to maintain an advantageous competition in the business — an alternative very perplexing to all
but men of exact probity, who are thereby
rendered, in a great measure, victims to a principle of legislation which does not sufficiently
accord with the bias of human nature. And
thus the laws become sources of discouragement
and loss to honest industry, and of profit and
advantage to perjury and fraud. It is a truth
that cannot be kept too constantly in view, that
all revenue laws which are so constructed as to
involve a lax and defective execution, are instruments of oppression to the most meritori-
ous part of those on whom they immediately
operate, and of additional burthens on the community at large. — *Report on Public Credit*,
1790. Vol. II, pp. 156–157.

HAMILTONIAN PRINCIPLES

Moral Duty of Governments

The principle which shall be assumed here is this, that the established *rules of morality and justice are applicable to nations as well as to individuals;* that the *former* as well as the *latter* are bound *to keep their promises; to fulfill their engagements to respect the rights of property* which others have acquired under contracts with them. Without this there is an end of all distinct ideas of right or wrong, justice or injustice, in relation to society or government. There can be no such thing as rights, no such thing as property or liberty; all the boasted advantages of a constitution of government vanish into air. Every thing must float on the variable and vague opinions of the governing party, of whomsoever composed.

To this it may be answered that the doctrine, as a general one, is true, but that there are certain great cases which operate as exceptions to the rule, and in which the public good may demand and justify a departure from it.

It shall not be denied that there are such cases; but as the admission of them is one of the most common as well as the most fruitful sources of error and abuse, it is of the greatest importance that just ideas should be formed of their true nature, foundation, and extent. To minds which are either depraved or feeble, or under the influence of any particular passion or prejudice, it is enough that cases are only attended with some *extraordinary circumstances* to induce their being considered as among the exceptions. *Convenience* is with them a substitute for *necessity*, and some temporary, partial advantage is an equivalent for a fundamental and permanent interest of society. We have too often seen in the United States examples of this species of levity. The treaties of the United States, the sacred rights of private property, have been too frequently sported with, from a too great facility in admitting exceptions to the maxims of public faith and the general rules of property. A desire to escape from this evil was a principal cause of the union which took place among good men to establish the national government; and it behoved its friends to have been particularly cautious how they set an example of equal relaxation in the practice of that very government.

The characteristics of the only admissible exceptions to the principle that has been assumed, are 1st. *Necessity*. 2d. There being some intrinsic and inherent quality in the thing which is to constitute the exception, contrary to the social order and to the permanent good of society.

Necessity is admitted in all moral reasoning as an exception to general rules. It is of two kinds, as applied to nations — where there is want of ability to perform a duty, and then it is involuntary; and where the general rule cannot be observed without some *manifest* and *great* national calamity.

If from extraordinary circumstances a nation is disabled from performing its stipulations, or its duty in any other respect, it is then excusable on the score of inability. But the inability must be a real, not a pretended, one; one that has been experimentally ascertained, or that can be demonstrated to the satisfaction of all honest and discerning men. And the deviation ought to be as small as possible; all that is practicable ought to be done.

A nation is alike excusable in certain extraordinary cases for not observing a right in performing a duty, if the one or the other would involve a *manifest* and *great* national calamity. But here, also, an extreme case is intended; the calamity to be avoided must not only be evident and considerable — it must be such an one as is like to prove fatal to the nation — as threatens its existence, or at least its permanent welfare.

War, for instance, is almost always a national calamity, of a serious kind; but it ought often to be encountered in protection *even* of a part of the community injured or annoyed; or in performance of the condition of a defensive alliance with some other nation.

But if such special circumstances exist in either case, that the going to war would eminently endanger the existence or permanent welfare of the nation, it may excusably be forborne.

Of the second class of exceptions, the case of certain feudal rights, which once oppressed all Europe, and still oppress too great a part of it, may serve as an example; rights which made absolute slaves of a part of the community, and rendered the condition of the greatest proportion of the remainder not much more eligible.

These rights, though involving that of property, being contrary to the social order, and to the permanent welfare of society, were justifiably abolished in the instances, in which abolitions have taken place, and may be abolished in all the remaining vestiges.

HAMILTONIAN PRINCIPLES

Wherever, indeed, a right of property is infringed for the general good, if the nature of the case admits of compensation, it ought to be made; but if compensation be impracticable, that impracticality ought not to be an obstacle to a clearly essential reform. — *Vindication of the Funding System*, 1791 [?]. Vol. II, pp. 295–298.

INTERNATIONAL MORALITY

It may be affirmed as a general principle, that the predominant motive of good offices from one nation to another, is the interest or advantage of the nation which performs them.

Indeed, the rule of morality in this respect is not precisely the same between nations as between individuals. The duty of making its own welfare the guide of its actions, is much stronger upon the former than upon the latter; in proportion to the greater magnitude and importance of national compared with individual happiness, and to the greater permanency of the effects of national than of individual conduct. Existing millions, and for the most part future generations, are concerned in the present measures of a government; while the consequences of the private actions of an individual ordinarily terminate with himself, or are circumscribed within a narrow compass.

Whence it follows that an individual may, on numerous occasions, meritoriously indulge the emotions of generosity and benevolence, not only without an eye to, but even at the expense of, his own interest. But a government can rarely, if at all, be justifiable in pursuing a similar course; and, if it does so, ought to confine itself within much stricter bounds. Good offices which are indifferent to the interest of a nation performing them, or which are compensated by the existence or expectation of some reasonable equivalent, or which produce an essential good to the nation to which they are rendered, without real detriment to the affairs of the benefactors, prescribe perhaps the limits of national generosity or benevolence.

It is not here meant to recommend a policy absolutely selfish or interested in nations; but to show, that a policy regulated by their own interest, as far as justice and good faith permit, is, and ought to be, their prevailing one; and that either to ascribe to them a different principle of action, or to deduce, from the supposition of it, arguments for a self-denying and self-sacrificing gratitude on the part of a nation which may have received from another good offices, is to misrepresent or misconceive what usually are, and ought to be, the springs of national conduct. — *"Pacificus,"* 1793. Vol. IV, pp. 166–167.

UNITARY AND FEDERAL STATES

In a single state where the sovereign power is exercised by delegation, whether it be a limited monarchy or a republic, the danger most commonly is, that the sovereign will become too powerful for his constituents. In federal governments, where different states are represented in a general council, the danger is on the other side — that the members will be an overmatch for the common head; or, in other words, that it will not have sufficient influence and authority to secure the obedience of the several parts of the confederacy.

In a single state the sovereign has the whole legislative power as well as the command of the national forces — of course an immediate control over the persons and property of the subjects; every other power is subordinate and dependent. If he undertakes to subvert the constitution, it can only be preserved by a general insurrection of the people. The magistrates of the provinces, counties, or towns into which the State is divided, having only an executive and police jurisdiction, can take no decisive measures for counteracting the first indications of tyranny; but must content themselves with the ineffectual weapon of petition and remonstrance. They cannot raise money, levy troops, nor form alliances. The leaders of the people must wait till their discontents have ripened into a general revolt, to put them in a situation to confer the powers necessary for their defence. It will always be difficult for this to take place; because the sovereign, possessing the appearance and forms of legal authority, having the forces and revenues of the state at his command, and a large party among the people besides, — which with those advantages he can hardly fail to acquire — he will too often be able to baffle the first motions of the discontented, and prevent that union and concert essential to the success of their opposition.

The security, therefore, of the public liberty must consist in such a distribution of the sovereign power, as will make it morally impossible for one part to gain an ascendency over the other, or for the whole to unite in a scheme of usurpation. — *The Continentalist*, July 19, 1781. Vol. I, pp. 236–237.

CONSTITUTIONS

Constitutions should consist only of general provisions; the reason is that they must necessarily be permanent, and that they cannot calculate for the possible change of things. — *Speech on the Senate of the United States*, June 28, 1788. Vol. I, p. 486.

REPUBLICANISM

I said that I was affectionately attached to the republican theory. This is the real language of my heart, which I open to you in the sincerity of friendship; and I add that I have strong hopes of the success of that theory; but, in candor, I ought also to add that I am far from being without doubts. I consider its success as yet a problem. It is yet to be determined by experience whether it be consistent with that stability and order in government which are essential to public strength and private security and happiness.

On the whole, the only enemy which Republicanism has to fear in this country is in the spirit of faction and anarchy. If this will not permit the ends of government to be attained under it, if it engenders disorders in the community, all regular and orderly minds will wish for a change, and the demagogues who have produced the disorder will make it for their own aggrandizement. This is the old story. If I were disposed to promote monarchy and overthrow State governments, I would mount the hobby-horse of popularity; I would cry out "usurpation," "danger to liberty," etc., etc.; I would endeavor to prostrate the national government, raise a ferment, and then "ride in the whirlwind, and direct the storm." That there are men acting with Jefferson and Madison who have this view, I verily believe; I could lay my finger on some of them. That Madison does not mean it, I also verily believe; and I rather believe the same of Jefferson, but I read him upon the whole thus: "A man of profound ambition and violent passions." — *Letter to Colonel Edward Carrington*, 1792. Vol. VIII, p. 264.

THE PEOPLE

THE PEOPLE

Their Passions

In all general questions which become the subjects of discussion, there are always some truths mixed with falsehoods. I confess, there is danger where men are capable of holding two offices. Take mankind in general, they are vicious, their passions may be operated upon. We have been taught to reprobate the danger of influence in the British government, without duly reflecting how far it was necessary to support a good government. We have taken up many ideas upon trust, and at last, pleased with our own opinions, establish them as undoubted truths. Hume's opinion of the British constitution confirms the remark, that there is always a body of firm patriots, who often shake a corrupt administration. Take mankind as they are, and what are they governed by? Their passions. There may be in every government a few choice spirits, who may act from more worthy motives. One great error is that we suppose mankind more honest than they are. Our prevailing passions are ambition and interest; and it will ever be the duty of a wise government to avail itself of the passions, in order to make them subservient to the public good; for these ever induce us to action. Perhaps a few men in a State may, from patriotic motives, or to display their talents, or to reap the advantage of public applause, step forward; but, if we adopt the clause [forbidding representatives to hold other office], we destroy the motive. I am, therefore, against all exclusions and refinements, except only in this case: that, when a member takes his seat, he should vacate every other office. — *Speech in the Federal Convention*, June 22, 1787. Vol. I, p. 389.

Their Errors

There are some who would be inclined to regard the servile pliancy of the Executive to a prevailing current, either in the community or in the legislature, as its best recommendation. But such men entertain very crude notions, as well of the purposes for which government was instituted, as of the true means by which the public happiness may be promoted. The republican principle demands that the deliberate sense of the community should govern the conduct of those to whom they intrust the management of their affairs; but it does not require an unqualified complaisance to every sudden breeze of passion, or to every transient impulse which the people may receive from the arts of men, who flatter their prejudices to betray their interests. It is a just observation, that the people commonly *intend* the *public good*. This often applies to their very errors. But their good sense would despise the adulator who should pretend that they always *reason right* about the *means* of promoting it. They know from experience that they sometimes err; and the wonder is that they so seldom err as they do, beset, as they continually are, by the wiles of parasites and sycophants, by the snares of the ambitious, the avaricious, the desperate, by the artifices of men who possess their confidence more than they deserve it, and of those who seek to possess rather than to deserve it. When occasions present themselves, in which the interests of the people are at variance with their inclinations, it is the duty of the persons whom they have appointed to be the guardians of those interests, to withstand the temporary delusion, in order to give them time and opportunity for more cool and sedate reflection. — *The Federalist.* Vol. IX, pp. 446–447.

Their Turbulence

All communities divide themselves into the few and the many. The first are the rich and well-born, the other the mass of the people. The voice of the people has been said to be the voice of God; and, however generally this maxim has been quoted and believed, it is not true to fact. The people are turbulent and changing; they seldom judge or determine right. Give, therefore, to the first class a distinct, permanent share in the government. They will check the unsteadiness of the second, and, as they cannot receive any advantage by a change, they therefore will ever maintain good government. Can a democratic Assembly, who annually revolve in the mass of the people, be supposed steadily to pursue the public good? Nothing but a permanent body can check the imprudence of democracy. Their turbulent and uncontrolling disposition requires checks. The Senate of New York, although chosen for four years, we have found to be inefficient. Will, on the Virginia plan, a continuance of seven years do it? It is admitted, that you cannot have a good Executive upon a democratic plan. See the excellency of the British Executive. He is placed above temptation. He can have no distinct interests from the public welfare. Nothing short of such an executive can be efficient. The weak side of a republican government is the danger of foreign influence. This is unavoidable, unless it is so constructed as to bring forward its first characters in its support. — *Speech in the Federal Convention*, June 18, 1787.   Vol. I, pp. 381–383.

The Governing and the Governed

It has been often asserted, that the interests of the general and of State Legislatures are precisely the same. This cannot be true. The views of the governed are often materially different from those who govern. The Science of policy is the knowledge of human nature. A State government will ever be the rival power of the general government. It is therefore highly improper that the State Legislatures should be the paymasters of the members of the national government. All political bodies love power, and it will often be improperly attained. — *Speech in the Federal Convention*, as reported by Yates, June 22, 1787.   Vol. I, p. 388.

HAMILTONIAN PRINCIPLES

The Fundamental Social Distinction

Hamilton acknowledged himself not to think favorably of republican government; but addressed his remarks to those who did think favorably of it, in order to prevail on them to tone their government as high as possible. He professed himself to be as zealous an advocate for liberty as any man whatever; and trusted he should be as willing a martyr to it, though he differed as to the form in which it was most eligible. He concurred, also, in the general observations of Mr. Madison on the subject, which might be supported by others if it were necessary. It was certainly true, that nothing like an equality of property existed; that an inequality would exist as long as liberty existed, and that it would unavoidably result from that very liberty itself. This inequality of property constituted the great and fundamental distinction in society. When the tribunitial power had levelled the boundary between the patricians and the plebeians, what followed? The distinction between rich and poor was substituted. — *Speeches in the Federal Convention*, as reported in the *Madison Papers*, June 22, 1787. Vol. I, p. 390.

HAMILTONIAN PRINCIPLES

THE DANGER OF DEMOCRACY

We are now forming a republican government. Real liberty is never found in despotism or the extremes of democracy, but in moderate governments. Those who mean to form a solid republican government ought to proceed to the confines of another government. As long as offices are open to all men, and no constitutional rank is established, it is pure republicanism. But if we *incline too much to democracy, we shall soon shoot into a monarchy. — Speeches in the Federal Convention*, as reported by Yates, June 26, 1787. Vol. I, p. 391.

It has been observed that a pure democracy, if it were practicable, would be the most perfect government. Experience has proved, that no position in politics is more false than this. The ancient democracies, in which the people themselves deliberated, never possessed one feature of good government. Their very character was tyranny; their figure deformity. When they assembled, the field of debate presented an ungovernable mob, not only incapable of deliberation, but prepared for every enormity. In these assemblies the enemies of the people brought forward their plans of ambition systematically. They were opposed by their enemies of another party; and it became a matter of contingency, whether the people subjected themselves to be led blindly by one tyrant or by another.

It was remarked yesterday that a numerous representation was necessary to obtain the confidence of the people. This is not generally true. The confidence of the people will easily be gained by a good administration. This is the true touchstone. — *Speech on the Compromises of the Constitution*, June 21, 1788. Vol. I, p. 431.

The Influence of Riches

While property continues to be pretty equally divided, and a considerable share of information pervades the community, the tendency of the people's suffrages will be to elevate merit even from obscurity. As riches increase and accumulate in few hands, as luxury prevails in society, virtue will be in a greater degree considered as only a graceful appendage of wealth, and the tendency of things will be to depart from the republican standard. This is the real disposition of human nature; it is what neither

the honorable member nor myself can correct.
It is a common misfortune that awaits our
State constitution, as well as all others. —
Speech on the Compromises of the Constitution,
June 21, 1788.   Vol. I, p. 435.

Social Classes

It is a harsh doctrine, that men grow wicked
in proportion as they improve and enlighten
their minds.   Experience has by no means justified us in the supposition that there is more
virtue in one class of men than in another.
Look through the rich and the poor of the community; the learned and the ignorant.   Where
does virtue predominate?   The difference indeed consists, not in the quantity, but kind of
vices, which are incident to the various classes;
and here the advantage of character belongs to
the wealthy.   Their vices are probably more
favorable to the prosperity of the State than
those of the indigent, and partake less of moral
depravity. — *Speeches on the Compromises of
the Constitution*, June 21, 1788.   Vol. I, p. 436.

Necessity of Checking the People

It is an unquestionable truth, that the body
of the people in every country desire sincerely

its prosperity.   But it is equally unquestionable that they do not possess the discernment and stability necessary for systematic government. To deny that they are frequently led into the grossest errors, by misinformation and passion, would be a flattery which their own good sense must despise.   That branch of administration, especially, which involves our political relation with foreign states, a community will ever be incompetent to.   These truths are not often held up in public assemblies; but they cannot be unknown to any who hear me.   From these principles, it follows that there ought to be two distinct bodies in our government: one which shall be immediately constituted by and peculiarly represent the people and possess all the popular features; another formed upon the principles and for the purposes before explained. Such considerations as these induce the convention who formed your State constitution to institute a Senate upon the present plan.   The history of ancient and modern republics had taught them that many of the evils which those republics suffered arose from the want of a certain balance, and that mutual control indispensable to a wise administration.   They were convinced that popular assemblies are frequently misguided by ignorance, by sudden impulses, and the intrigues of ambitious men; and that some firm barrier against these operations was necessary. They, therefore, instituted your Senate; and the benefits we have experienced have fully justified their conceptions. — *Speech on the Senate of the United States*, June 24, 1788, as given in *Elliot's Debates*. Vol. I, pp. 450–451.

REPRESENTATION OF CLASSES

The subject [number and nature of representatives] might be placed in several other lights that would all lead to the same result; and in particular it might be asked, What greater affinity or relation of interest can be conceived between the carpenter and blacksmith, and the linen manufacturer or stocking weaver, than between the merchant and either of them? It is notorious that there are often as great rivalships between different branches of the mechanic or manufacturing arts as there are between any of the departments of labor and industry; so that, unless the representative body were to be far more numerous than would be consistent with any idea of regularity or wisdom in its deliberations, it is impossible that what seems to be the spirit of the objection we have been considering should ever be realized in practice.—*The Federalist.* Vol. IX, p. 208.

SECURITY OF THE RIGHTS OF GROUPS

In a single republic, all the power surrendered by the people is submitted to the administration of a single government; and the usurpations are guarded against by a division of the government into distinct and separate departments. In the compound republic of America, the power surrendered by the people is first divided between two distinct governments, and then the portion allotted to each subdivided among distinct and separate departments. Hence a double security arises to the rights of the people. The different governments will control each other, at the same time that each will be controlled by itself.

It is of great importance in a republic not only to guard against the oppression of its rulers, but to guard one part of society against the injustice of the other part. Different interests necessarily exist in different classes of citizens. If a majority be united by a common interest, the rights of the minority will be insecure. There are but two methods of providing against this evil: the one by creating a will in the community independent of the majority — that is, of the society itself; the other, by comprehending in the society so many separate descriptions of citizens as will render an unjust combination of a majority of the whole very improbable, if not impracticable. The first method prevails in all governments possessing an hereditary or self-appointed authority. This, at best, is but a precarious security; because a power independent of the society may as well espouse the unjust views of the major, as the rightful interests of the minor party, and may possibly be turned against both parties. The second method will be exemplified in the federal republic of the United States. Whilst all authority in it will be derived from and dependent on the society, the society itself will be broken into so many parts, interests, and classes of citizens, that the rights of individuals, or of the minority, will be in little danger from interested combinations of the majority. In a free government the security for civil rights must be the same as that for religious rights. It consists in the one case in the multiplicity of interests, and in the other in the multiplicity of sects. The degree of security in both cases will depend

on the number of interests and sects; and this
may be presumed to depend on the extent of
country and number of people comprehended
under the same government. This view of the
subject must particularly recommend a proper
federal system to all the sincere and considerate
friends of republican government, since it shows
that in exact proportion as the territory of the
Union may be formed into more circumscribed
Confederacies, or States, oppressive combinations of a majority will be facilitated; the best
security, under the republican forms, for the
rights of every class of citizens, will be diminished; and consequently the stability and
independence of some member of the government, the only other security, must be propor-
tionally increased. — *The Federalist.* Vol. IX,
pp. 325-326.

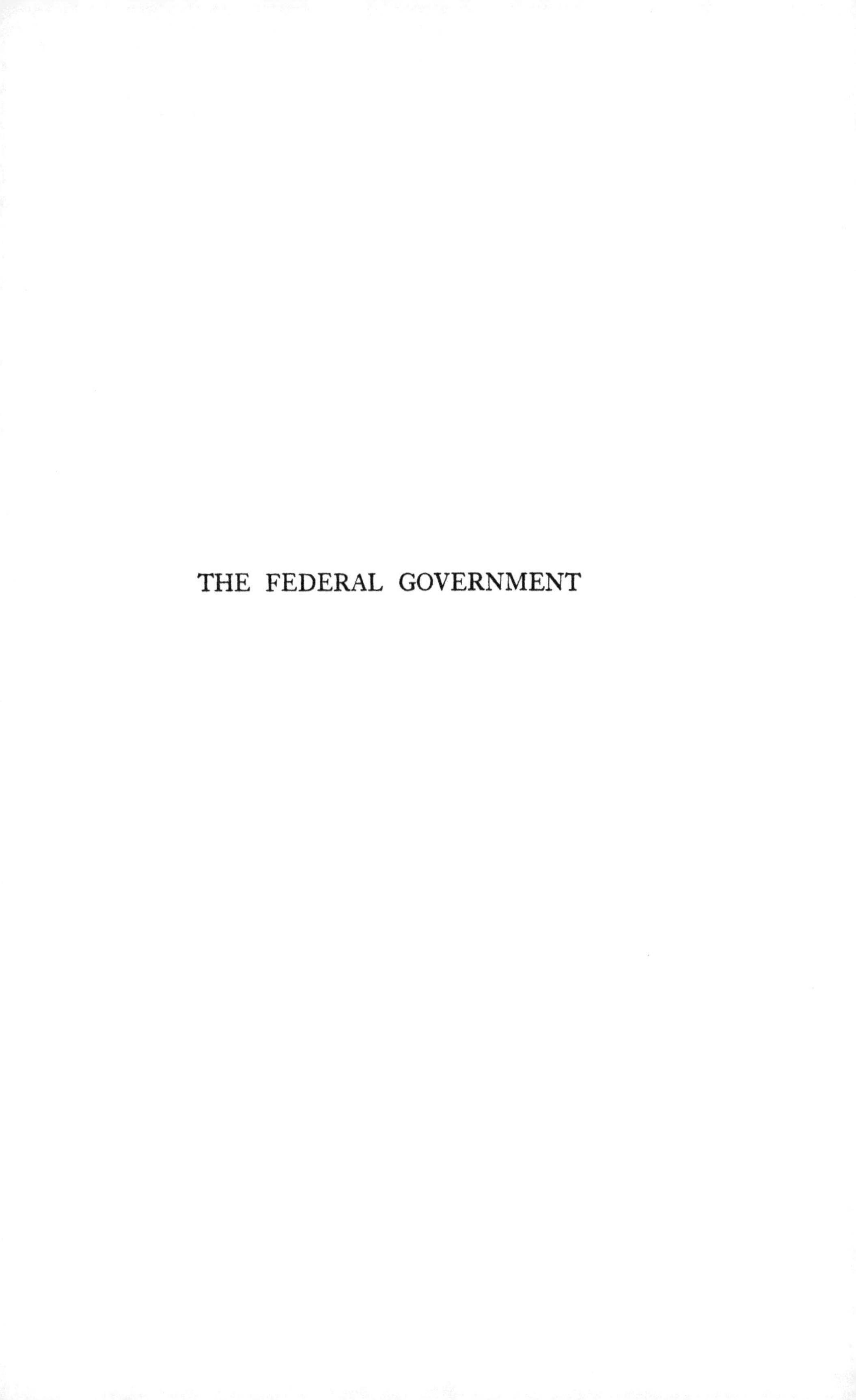

THE FEDERAL GOVERNMENT

THE FEDERAL GOVERNMENT

This *general principle* is *inherent* in the very *definition* of government, and *essential* to every step of the progress to be made by that of the United States, namely: That every power vested in a government is in its nature *sovereign*, and includes, by *force* of the *term*, a right to employ all the *means* requisite and fairly applicable to the attainment of the *ends* of such power, and which are not precluded by restrictions and exceptions specified in the Constitution, or not immoral, or not contrary to the *essential ends* of political society.

This principle, in its application to government in general, would be admitted as an axiom; and it will be incumbent upon those who may incline to deny it, to prove a distinction, and to show that a rule which, in the general system of things, is essential to the preservation of the social order, is inapplicable to the United States.

The circumstance that the powers of sovereignty are in this country divided between the National and State governments, does not afford the distinction required. It does not follow from this, that each of the portion of *powers* delegated to the one or the other, is not sovereign with *regard to its proper objects*. It will only *follow* from it, that each has sovereign power as to *certain things*, and not as to *other things*. To deny that the Government of the United States has sovereign power, as to its declared purposes and trusts, because its power does not extend to all cases, would be equally to deny that the State governments have sovereign power in any case, because their power does not extend to every case. The tenth section of the first article of the Constitution exhibits a long list of very important things which they may not do. And thus the United States would furnish the singular spectacle of a *political society* without *sovereignty*, or of a *people governed*, without *government*.

If it would be necessary to bring proof to a proposition so clear, as that which affirms that the powers of the Federal Government, as to *its objects*, were sovereign, there is a clause of its Constitution which would be decisive. It is that which declares that the Constitution, and the laws of the United States made in pursuance of it, and all treaties made, or which shall be made, under their authority, shall be the *supreme law of the land.* The power which can create the *supreme law of the land* in *any case*, is doubtless *sovereign* as to such case.

This general and indisputable principle puts at once an end to the *abstract* question, whether the United States have power to erect a *corporation;* that is to say, to give a *legal* or *artificial capacity* to one or more persons, distinct from the *natural.* But it is unquestionably incident to *sovereign power* to erect corporations, and consequently to *that* of the United States, in *relation* to the *objects* intrusted to the management of the government. The difference is this : where the authority of the government is general, it can create corporations in *all cases;* where it is confined to certain branches of legislation, it can create corporations *only* in those cases. — *Letter to Robert Morris*, 1780. Vol. III, pp. 181–182.

Powers of Government

After all our doubts, our suspicions, and speculations on the subject of government, we must return at last to the important truth, that when we have formed a Constitution upon free principles, when we have given a proper balance to the different branches of administration, and fixed representation upon pure and equal principles, we may with safety furnish it with all the powers necessary to answer in the most ample manner the purposes of government. The great desiderata are a free representation and mutual checks. When these are obtained, all our apprehensions of the extent of powers are unjust and imaginary. — *Speech on the Senate of the United States*, June 27, 1788. Vol. I, pp. 466–467.

Where ought the great resources to be lodged? Every rational man will give an immediate answer. To what extent shall these resources be possessed? Reason says, as far as possible exigencies can require; that is, without limitation. A constitution cannot set bounds to a nation's wants; it ought not therefore to set bounds to its resources. Unexpected visitations, long and ruinous wars, may demand all the possible abilities of the country. Shall not our government have power to call these abilities into action? The contingencies of society are not reducible to calculations; they cannot be fixed or bounded, even in imagination. Will you limit the means of your defence when you cannot ascertain the force or extent of the invasion ? — *Speech on the Senate of the United States,* June 27, 1788. Vol. I, pp. 471–472.

The authorities essential to the common defence are these: to raise armies; to build and equip fleets; to prescribe rules for the government of both; to direct their operations; to provide for their support. These powers ought to exist without limitation, *because it is impossible to foresee or define the extent and variety of national exigencies, or the correspondent extent and variety of the means which may be necessary to satisfy them.* The circumstances that endanger the safety of nations are infinite, and for this reason no constitutional shackles can wisely be imposed on the power to which the case is committed. This power ought to be co-extensive with all the possible combinations of such circumstances; and ought to be under the direction of the same councils which are appointed to preside over the common defence.

This is one of those truths which, to a correct and unprejudiced mind, carries its own evidence along with it; and may be obscured, but cannot be made plainer by argument or reasoning. It rests upon axioms as simple as they are universal; the *means* ought to be proportioned to the *end;* the persons, from whose agency the attainment of any *end* is expected, ought to possess the *means* by which it is to be attained.

Whether there ought to be a federal government intrusted with the care of the common defence, is a question in the first instance, open for discussion; but the moment it is decided in the affirmative, it will follow, that that government ought to be clothed with all the powers requisite to complete execution of its trust. And unless it can be shown that the circumstances which may affect the public safety are reducible within certain determinate limits; unless the contrary of this position can be fairly and rationally disputed, it must be admitted, as a necessary consequence, that there can be no limitation of that authority which is to provide for the defence and protection of the community, in any matter essential to its efficacy — that is, in any matter essential to the *formation, direction,* or *support* of the *national forces. — The Federalist.* Vol. IX, pp. 136–137.

HAMILTONIAN PRINCIPLES

I will, in this place, hazard an observation, which will not be the less just because to some it may appear new; which is, that the more the operations of the national authority are intermingled in the ordinary exercise of government, the more the citizens are accustomed to meet with it in the common occurrences of their political life, the more it is familiarized to their sight and to their feelings, the further it enters into those objects which touch the most sensible chords and put in motion the most active springs of the human heart, the greater will be the probability that it will conciliate the respect and attachment of the community. Man is very much a creature of habit. A thing that rarely strikes his senses will generally have but little influence upon his mind. A government continually at a distance and out of sight can hardly be expected to interest the sensations of the people. The inference is, that the authority of the Union, and the affections of the citizens towards it, will be strengthened, rather than weakened, by its extension to what are called matters of internal concern; and will have less occasion to recur to force, in proportion to the familiarity and comprehensiveness of its agency. The more it circulates through

those channels and currents in which the passions of mankind naturally flow, the less will it
require the aid of the violent and perilous expedients of compulsion. — *The Federalist.* Vol.
IX, p. 161.

A government ought to contain in itself every
power requisite to the full accomplishment of
the objects committed to its care, and to the
complete execution of the trusts for which it is
responsible, free from every other control but a
regard to the public good and to the sense of
the people.

As the duties of superintending the national
defence and of securing the public peace against
foreign or domestic violence involve a provision
for casualties and dangers to which no possible
limits can be assigned, the power of making
that provision ought to know no other bounds
than the exigencies of the nation and the resources of the community.

As revenue is the essential engine by which
the means of answering the national exigencies
must be procured, the power of procuring that
article in its full extent must necessarily be
comprehended in that of providing for those
exigencies.

As theory and practice conspire to prove that

the power of procuring revenue is unavailing when exercised over the States in their collective capacities, the federal government must of necessity be invested with an unqualified power of taxation in the ordinary modes. — *The Federalist.*   Vol. IX, p. 182.

A Strong Central Government

To the care of the Federal Government are confided directly, those great, general interests on which all particular interests materially depend: our safety in respect to foreign nations; our tranquillity in respect to each other; the foreign and mutual commerce of the States; the establishment and regulation of the money of the country; the management of our national finances; indirectly, the security of liberty by the guaranty of a republican form of government to each State; the security of property by interdicting any State from emitting paper money or from passing laws impairing the obligation of contracts (from both of which causes the rights of property had experienced serious injury); the prosperity of agriculture and manufactures, as intimately connected with that of commerce, and as depending in a variety of ways upon the agency of the General Government.

In fine, it is the province of the General Government to manage the greatest number of those concerns in which the provident activity and exertion of *government* are of most importance to the people; and we have only to compare the state of our country antecedent to the establishment of the Federal Constitution, with what it has been since, to be convinced that the most operative causes of the public prosperity depend upon that Constitution. It is not meant, by what has been said, to insinuate that the State governments are not extremely useful in their proper spheres; but the object is to guard against the mischiefs of exaggerating their importance, in derogation from that of the general right. Every attempt to do this, is, remotely, a stab at the union of these States; a blow to our collective existence as one people — and to all the blessings which are interwoven with that sacred fraternity.

If it be true, as insinuated, that "our organization is too complicated — too expensive," let it be simplified; let this, however, be done in such a manner as not to mutilate, weaken, and eventually destroy, our present system, but to increase the energy and insure the duration of our National Government — *the rock of our*

political salvation. — "Lucius Crassus," 1802.
Vol. VII, pp. 247-248.

Implied Powers

The foundation of the Constitution is laid on this ground: "That all powers not delegated to the United States by the Constitution, nor prohibited to it by the States, are reserved to the States, or to the people." Whence it is meant to be inferred, that Congress can in no case exercise any power not included in those enumerated in the Constitution. And it is affirmed, that the power of erecting a corporation is not included in any of the enumerated powers.

The main proposition here laid down, in its true significance, is not to be questioned. It is nothing more than a consequence of this republican maxim, that all government is a delegation of power. But how much is delegated in each case is a question of fact, to be made out by fair reasoning and construction, upon the particular provisions of the Constitution, taking as guides the general principles and general ends of governments.

It is not denied that there are *implied*, as well as *express powers*, and that the *former* are as effectually delegated as the *latter*. And for the sake of accuracy it shall be mentioned that there is another class of powers, which may be properly denominated *resulting powers*. It will not be doubted that if the United States should make a conquest of any of the territories of its neighbors, they would possess sovereign jurisdiction over the conquered territory. This would be rather a result from the whole mass of the powers of the government, and from the nature of political society, than a consequence of either of the powers specially enumerated.

But be this as it may, it furnishes a striking illustration of the general doctrine contended for; it shows an extensive case, in which a power of erecting corporations is either implied in, or would result from, some or all of the powers vested in the National Government. The jurisdiction acquired over such conquered country would certainly be competent to any species of legislation.

To return: — It is conceded that *implied powers* are to be considered as delegated equally with *express ones*. Then it follows, that as a power of erecting a corporation may as well be *implied* as any other thing, it may as well be employed as an *instrument* or *means* of carrying into execution any of the specified powers, as any other *instrument* or *means* whatever. The only question must be in this, as in every other case, whether the means to be employed, or, in this instance, the corporation to be erected, has a lawful relation to any of the acknowledged objects or lawful ends of the government. Thus a corporation may not be erected by Congress for superintending the police of the city of Philadelphia, because they are not authorized to *regulate* the *police* of that city. But one may be erected in relation to the collection of taxes, or to the trade with foreign countries, or to the trade between the States, or with the Indian tribes; because it is the province of the Federal Government to *regulate* those objects, and because it is incident to a general *sovereign* or *legislative* power to *regulate* a thing, to employ all the means which relate to its regulation to the best and greatest advantage. — *Letter to Robert Morris*, 1780. Vol. III, pp. 183–185.

Through this mode of reasoning respecting the right of employing all the means requisite to the execution of the specified powers of the government, it is objected, that none but necessary and proper means are to be employed;

and the Secretary of State [Jefferson] maintains, that no means are to be considered *necessary* but those without which the grant of the power would be *nugatory*. Nay, so far does he go in his restrictive interpretation of the *word*, as even to make the case of *necessity* which shall warrant the constitutional exercise of the power to depend on *casual* and *temporary* circumstances; an idea which alone refutes the construction. The *expediency* of exercising a particular power, at a particular time, must, indeed, depend on circumstances; but the constitutional right of exercising it must be uniform and invariable, the same today as to-morrow. . . .

It is essential to the being of the national government, that so erroneous a conception of the meaning of the word *necessary* should be exploded. It is certain, that neither the grammatical nor popular sense of the term requires that construction. According to both, *necessary* often means no more than *needful, requisite, incidental, useful,* or *conducive to.* It is a common mode of expression to say, that it is *necessary* for a government or a person to do this or that thing, when nothing more is intended or understood, than that the interests of the government or person require, or will be promoted by, the doing of this or that thing. The imagination can be at no loss for exemplifications of the use of the word in this sense. And it is the true one in which it is to be understood as used in the Constitution. The whole turn of the clause containing it indicates, that it was the intent of the Convention, by that clause, to give a liberal latitude to the exercise of the specified powers. The expressions have peculiar comprehensiveness. They are, "to make all *laws* necessary and proper for *carrying into execution* the *foregoing powers,* and *all other powers* vested by the Constitution in the *Government* of the United States, or in any *department* or *officer* thereof."

To understand the word as the Secretary of State does, would be to depart from its obvious and popular sense, and to give it a restrictive operation, an idea never before entertained. It would be to give it the same force as if the word *absolutely* or *indispensably* had been prefixed to it. . . .

The degree in which a measure is necessary can never be a *test* of the legal right to adopt it; that must be a matter of opinion, and can only be a *test* of expediency. The *relation* between the *measure* and the *end;* between the *nature* of the *means* employed toward the execution of a power, and the object of that power, must be the criterion of constitutionality, not the more or less of *necessity* or *utility*.

The practice of the government is against the rule of construction advocated by the Secretary of State. Of this, the act concerning lighthouses, beacons, buoys, and public piers is a decisive example. This, doubtless, must be referred to the powers of regulating trade, and is fairly relative to it. But it cannot be affirmed that the exercise of that power in this instance was strictly *necessary*, or that the power itself would be *nugatory*, without that of regulating establishments of this nature.

This restrictive interpretation of the word *necessary* is also contrary to this sound maxim of construction; namely, that the powers contained in a constitution of government, especially those which concern the general administration of the affairs of a country, its finances, trade, defence, etc., ought to be construed liberally in advancement of the public good. This rule does not depend on the particular form of a government, or on the particular demarcation of the boundaries of its powers, but on the nature and objects of government. . . .

HAMILTONIAN PRINCIPLES

An adherence to the letter of its powers would at once arrest the motions of government. — *Letter to Robert Morris*, 1780. Vol. III, pp. 186–191.

On the Division of Powers

The power of legislation is, in its own nature, the most comprehensive and potent of the three great subdivisions of sovereignty. It is the will of the government; it prescribes universally the rule of action, and the sanctions which are to enforce it. It creates and regulates the public force, and it commands the public purse. If deposited in an elective representative of the people, it has, in most cases, the body of the nation for its auxiliary, and generally acts with all the momentum of popular favor. In every such government it is consequently an organ of immense strength. But when there is an hereditary chief magistrate, clothed with dazzling prerogatives and a great patronage, there is a powerful counterpoise, which, in most cases, is sufficient to preserve the equilibrium of the government; in some cases, to incline the scales too much to its own side.

In governments wholly popular or representative, there is no adequate counterpoise.

HAMILTONIAN PRINCIPLES

Confidence in the most numerous, or legislative department, and jealousy of the executive chief, form the genius of every such government. That jealousy, operating in the constitution of the executive, causes the organ to be intrinsically feeble; and withholding in the course of administration accessory means of force and influence, is for the most part vigilant to continue it in a state of impotence. The result is that the legislative body, in this species of government, possesses additional resources of power and weight; while the executive is rendered much too weak for competition; almost too weak for self-defence.

A third principle, not less well founded than the other two, is that the judiciary department is naturally the weakest of the three. The sources of strength to the legislative branches have been briefly delineated. The executive, by means of its several active powers, of the dispensation of honors and emoluments, and of the direction of the public force, is evidently the second in strength. The judiciary, on the other hand, can ordain nothing. It commands neither the purse nor the sword. It has scarcely any patronage. Its functions are not active but deliberative. Its main province is to declare the meaning of the laws; and, in extraordinary cases, it must even look up to the executive aid for the execution of its decisions. Its chief strength is in the veneration which it is able to inspire by the wisdom and the rectitude of its judgments. — *"Lucius Crassus,"* 1802.   Vol. VII, pp. 285–286.

Direct Action of Central Government on Citizens

It seems to require no pains to prove that the States ought not to prefer a national Constitution which could only be kept in motion by the instrumentality of a large army continually on foot to execute the ordinary requisitions or decrees of the government. And yet this is the plain alternative involved by those who wish to deny it the power of extending its operations to individuals. Such a scheme, if practicable at all, would instantly degenerate into a military despotism; but it will be found in every light impracticable. The resources of the Union would not be equal to the maintenance of an army considerable enough to confine the larger States within the limits of their duty; nor would the means ever be furnished of form-

ing such an army in the first instance. Whoever considers the populousness and strength of
several of these States singly at the present
juncture, and looks forward to what they will
become even at the distance of half a century,
will at once dismiss as idle and visionary any
scheme which aims at regulating their movements by laws to operate upon them in their
collective capacities, and to be executed by a
coercion applicable to them in the same capacities. A project of this kind is little less roman-
tic than the monster-taming spirit which is
attributed to the fabulous heroes and demi-gods
of antiquity. . . .

The result of these observations to an intel-
ligent mind must be clearly this, that if it be
possible at any rate to construct a federal government capable of regulating the common
concerns and preserving the general tranquillity . . . it must carry its agency to the persons
of the citizens. It must stand in need of no
intermediate legislations; but must itself be
empowered to employ the arm of the ordinary
magistrate to execute its own resolutions. The
majesty of the national authority must be
manifested through the medium of the courts
of justice. The government of the Union, like

that of each State, must be able to address itself immediately to the hopes and fears of individuals; and to attract to its support those passions which have the strongest influence upon the human heart. — *The Federalist.* Vol. IX, pp. 94–95.

THE STATE GOVERNMENTS

THE STATE GOVERNMENTS

IT is the temper of societies as well as of individuals to be impatient of constraint, and to prefer partial to general interest. Many cases may occur where members of a confederacy have, or seem to have, an advantage in things contrary to the good of the whole, or a disadvantage in others conducive to that end. The selfishness of every part will dispose each to believe that the public burdens are unequally apportioned, and that itself is the victim. These and other circumstances will promote a disposition for abridging the authority of the federal government; and the ambition of men in office in each state will make them glad to encourage it. They think their own consequence connected with the power of the government of which they are a part; and will endeavor to increase the one as the means of increasing the other.

The particular governments will have more empire over the minds of their subjects than the general one, because their agency will be more direct, more uniform, and more apparent. The people will be habituated to look up to them as the arbiters and guardians of their personal concerns, by which the passions of the vulgar, if not of all men, are most strongly affected; and in every difference with the confederated body, will side with them against the common sovereign. — *The Continentalist*, July 19, 1781. Vol. I, pp. 238–239.

INFLUENCE OF STATE GOVERNMENTS

The forms of our State constitutions must always give them great weight in our affairs, and will make it too difficult to bend them to the pursuit of a common interest, too easy to oppose whatever they do not like, and to form partial combinations subversive of the general one. There is a wide difference between our situation and that of an empire under one simple form of government, distributed into counties, provinces, or districts, which have no Legislatures, but merely magistratical bodies to execute the laws of a common sovereign. Here the danger is that the sovereign will have too much power, and oppress the parts of which it is composed. In our case, that of an empire composed of confederated States, each with a government completely organized within itself, having all the means to draw its subjects to a close dependence on itself, the danger is directly the reverse. It is that the common sovereign will not have power sufficient to unite the different members together, and direct the common forces to the interest and happiness of the whole. — *Letter to James Duane*, September 3, 1780. Vol. I, pp. 206–207.

STATE AND FEDERAL GOVERNMENTS

In a contest of this kind [between the Federal government and the states], the body of the people will always be on the side of the State governments. This will not only result from their love of liberty and regard to their own safety, but from other strong principles of human nature. The State governments operate on those immediate familiar personal concerns to which the sensibility of individuals is awake. The distribution of private justice belonging to them, they must always appear to the sense of the people as the immediate guardians of their rights. They will, of course, have the strongest hold on their attachment, respect, and obedience. Another circumstance will contribute to the same end. Far the greatest number of offices and employments are in the gift of the States separately; the weight of official influence will therefore be in favor of the State governments; and, with all these advantages, they cannot fail to carry the people along with them in every contest with the General Government in which they are not palpably in the wrong, and often when they are. What is to be feared from the efforts of Congress to establish a tyranny, with the great body of the people, under the direction of their State governments, combined in opposition to their views? Must not their attempts recoil upon themselves, and terminate in their own ruin and disgrace? or, rather, would not these considerations, if they were insensible to other motives, for ever restrain them from making such attempts?

The causes taken notice of, as securing the attachment of the people to their local governments, present us with another important truth — the natural imbecility of federal governments, and the danger that they will never be able to exercise power enough to manage the general affairs of the Union; though the States will have a common interest, yet they will also have a particular interest. For example, as a part of the Union, it will be the interest of every State to pay as little itself, and to let its neighbors pay as much as possible. Particular interests have always more influence upon men than general. The Federal States, therefore, consulting their immediate advantage, may be considered as so many eccentric powers, tending in a contrary direction to the government of the Union; and as they will generally carry the people along with them, the Confederacy will be in continual danger of dissolution. This, Mr. Chairman, is the real rock upon which the happiness of this country is likely to split. This is the point to which our fears and cares should be directed, to guard against this, and not to terrify ourselves with imaginary dangers from the spectre of power in Congress, will be our true wisdom. — *Speech on the Revenue System*, 1787. Vol. II, pp. 30–31.

As to the destruction of State governments, the great and real anxiety is to be able to preserve the national from the too potent and counteracting influence of those governments. As to my own political creed, I give it to you with the utmost sincerity. I am affectionately attached to the republican theory. I desire

above all things to see the equality of political
rights, exclusive of all hereditary distinction,
firmly established by a practical demonstration
of its being consistent with the order and happiness of society. As to State governments,
the prevailing bias of my judgment is that if
they can be circumscribed within bounds, consistent with the preservation of the national
government, they will prove useful and salutary.   If the States were all of the size of Con-
necticut, Maryland, or New Jersey, I should
decidedly regard the local governments as both
safe and useful.   As the thing now is, I acknowledge the most serious apprehensions, that the
government of the United States will not be
able to maintain itself against their influence.
I see that influence already penetrating into
the national councils and preventing their direction. Hence a disposition on my part towards
a liberal construction of the powers of the national government, and to erect every fence, to
guard it from depredations, which is, in my
opinion, consistent with constitutional propriety. As to any combination to prostrate
the State governments, I disavow and deny it.
— *Letter to Colonel Edward Carrington*, 1792.
Vol. VIII, pp. 263–264.

HAMILTONIAN PRINCIPLES

There is, in the nature of sovereign power, an impatience of control, that disposes those who are invested with the exercise of it, to look with an evil eye upon all external attempts to restrain or direct its operations. From this spirit it happens, that in every political association which is formed upon the principle of uniting in a common interest a number of lesser sovereignties, there will be found a kind of eccentric tendency in the subordinate or inferior orbs, by the operation of which there will be a perpetual effort in each to fly off from the common centre. This tendency is not difficult to be accounted for. It has its origin in the love of power. Power controlled or abridged is almost always the rival and enemy of that power by which it is controlled or abridged. This simple proposition will teach us, how little reason there is to expect, that the persons intrusted with the administration of the affairs of the particular members of a confederacy, will at all times be ready, with perfect good-humor, and an unbiased regard to the public weal, to execute the resolutions or decrees of the general authority. The reverse of this results from the constitution of human nature.

If, therefore, the measures of the Confederacy

cannot be executed without the intervention of the particular administrations, there will be little prospect of their being executed at all. The rulers of the respective members, whether they have a constitutional right to do it or not, will undertake to judge of the propriety of the measures themselves. They will consider the conformity of the thing proposed or required to their immediate interests or aims; the momentary conveniences or inconveniences that would attend its adoption. All this will be done; and in a spirit of interested and suspicious scrutiny, without that knowledge of national circumstances and reasons of state, which is essential to a right judgment, and with that strong predilection in favor of local objects, which can hardly fail to mislead the decision. The same process must be repeated in every member of which the body is constituted; and the execution of the plans, framed by the councils of the whole, will always fluctuate on the discretion of the ill-informed and prejudiced opinion of every part. Those who have been conversant in the proceedings of popular assemblies; who have seen how difficult it often is, where there is no exterior pressure of circumstances, to bring them to harmonious resolutions on important points, will readily conceive how impossible it must be to induce a number of such assemblies, deliberating at a distance from each other, at different times, and under different impressions, long to cooperate in the same views and pursuits. — *The Federalist.* Vol. IX, p. 90.

It is . . . improbable that there should exist a disposition in the federal councils to usurp the powers with which they are connected; because the attempt to exercise those powers would be as troublesome as it would be nugatory; and the possession of them, for that reason, would contribute nothing to the dignity, to the importance, or to the splendor of the national government. . . .

It will always be far more easy for the State governments to encroach upon the national authorities, than for the national government to encroach upon the State authorities. The proof of this proposition turns upon the greater degree of influence which the State governments, if they administer their affairs with uprightness and prudence, will generally possess over the people; a circumstance which at the same time teaches us that there is an inherent and intrinsic weakness in all federal constitutions; and that too much pains cannot be taken in their organization, to give them all the force which is compatible with the principles of liberty. . . .

It is a known fact in human nature, that its affections are commonly weak in proportion to the distance or diffusiveness of the object. Upon the same principle that a man is more attached to his family than to his neighborhood, to his neighborhood than to the community at large, the people of each State would be more apt to feel a stronger bias towards their local governments than towards the government of the Union; unless the force of that principle should be destroyed by a much better administration of the latter. . . .

There is one transcendent advantage belonging to the province of the State governments, which alone suffices to place the matter in a clear and satisfactory light, — I mean the ordinary administration of criminal and civil justice. This, of all others, is the most powerful, most universal, and most attractive source of popular obedience and attachment. — *The Federalist.* Vol. IX, pp. 98–99.

The moment we launch into conjectures about the usurpations of the federal government, we get into an unfathomable abyss, and fairly put ourselves out of the reach of all reasoning. Imagination may range at pleasure till it gets bewildered amidst the labyrinths of an enchanted castle, and knows not on which side to extricate itself from the perplexities into which it has so rashly adventured. Whatever may be the limits or modifications of the powers of the Union, it is easy to imagine an endless train of possible dangers; and by indulging an excess of jealousy and timidity, we may bring ourselves to a state of absolute scepticism and irresolution. I repeat here what I have observed in substance in another place, that all observations founded upon the danger of usurpation ought to be referred to the composition and structure of the government, not to the nature or extent of its powers. The State governments, by their original constitutions, are invested with complete sovereignty. In what does our security consist against usurpation from that quarter? Doubtless in the manner of their formation, and in a due dependence of those who are to administer them upon the people. If the proposed construction of the federal government be found, upon an impartial examination of it, to be such as to afford, to a proper extent, the same species of security, all apprehensions on the score of usurpation ought to be discarded.

It should not be forgotten that a disposition in the State governments to encroach upon the rights of the Union is quite as probable as a disposition in the Union to encroach upon the rights of the State governments. What side would be likely to prevail in such a conflict, must depend on the means which the contending parties could employ towards insuring success. As in republics, strength is always on the side of the people, and as there are weighty reasons to induce a belief that the State governments will commonly possess most influence over them, the natural conclusion is that such contests will be most apt to end to the disadvantage of the Union; and that there is greater probability of encroachments by the members upon the Federal head, than by the Federal head upon the members. But it is evident that all conjectures of this kind must be extremely vague and fallible; and that it is by far the safest course to lay them altogether aside, and to confine our attention wholly to the nature and ex-

tent of the powers as they are delineated in the
Constitution. Every thing beyond this must
be left to the prudence and firmness of the
people; who, as they will hold the scales in
their own hands, it is to be hoped, will always
take care to preserve the constitutional equilibrium between the general and the State
governments. Upon this ground, which is
evidently the true one, it will not be difficult
to obviate the objections which have been made
to an indefinite power of taxation in the United
States. — *The Federalist.*   Vol. IX, pp. 183–185.

THE PRESIDENT

THE PRESIDENT

MODE OF CHOOSING A PRESIDENT

IF the manner of it [the election of a President by electors] be not perfect, it is at least excellent. It unites in an eminent degree all the advantages, the union of which was to be wished for.

It was desirable that the sense of the people should operate in the choice of the person to whom so important a trust was to be confided. This end will be answered by committing the right of making it, not to any preestablished body, but to men chosen by the people for the special purpose, and at the particular conjuncture.

It was equally desirable, that the immediate election should be made by men most capable of analyzing the qualities adapted to the station, and acting under circumstances favorable to deliberation, and to a judicious combination of all the reasons, and inducements which were proper to govern their choice. A small number of persons, selected by their fellow-citizens from the general mass, will be most likely to possess the information and discernment requisite to such complicated investigations.

It was also desirable to afford as little opportunity as possible to tumult and disorder. This evil was not least to be dreaded in the election of a magistrate, who was to have so important an agency in the administration of the government as the President of the United States. But the precautions which have been so happily concerted in the system under consideration, promise an effectual security against this mischief. The choice of *several*, to form an intermediate body of electors, will be much less apt to convulse the community with any extraordinary or violent movements, than the choice of *one* who was himself to be the final object of the public wishes. And as the electors, chosen in each State, are to assemble and vote in the State in which they are chosen, this detached and divided situation will expose them much less to heats and ferments, which might be communicated from them to the people, than if they were all to be convened at one time, in one place. — *The Federalist*. Vol. IX, pp. 424–425.

HAMILTONIAN PRINCIPLES

The President and Central Government

I am . . . for a general government, yet would wish to go the full length of republican principles. Let one body of the Legislature be constituted during good behavior or life. Let an Executive be appointed who dares execute his powers. It may be asked: Is this a republican system? It is strictly so, as long as they remain elective. And let me observe, that an Executive is less dangerous to the liberties of the people when in office during life, than for seven years. It may be said, this constitutes an elective monarchy. Pray, what is a monarchy? May not the governors of the respective States be considered in that light? But, by making the Executive subject to impeachment, the term monarchy cannot apply. These elective monarchs have produced tumults in Rome, and are equally dangerous to peace in Poland; but this cannot apply to the mode in which I would propose the election. Let electors be appointed in each of the States to elect the Executive . . . [the Legislature] to consist of two branches; and I would give them the unlimited power of passing all laws, without exception. The Assembly to be elected for

three years, by the people in districts. The
Senate to be elected by electors to be chosen
for that purpose by the people, and to remain
in office during life. The Executive to have
the power of negativing all laws; to make war
or peace, with their advice, but to have the sole
direction of all military operations, and to send
ambassadors, and appoint all military officers;
and to pardon all offenders, treason excepted,
unless by advice of the Senate. On his death
or removal, the President of the Senate to
officiate, with the same powers, until another is
elected. Supreme judicial officers to be appointed by the Executive and the Senate. The
Legislature to appoint courts in each State, so
as to make the State governments unnecessary
to it. All State laws which contravene the
general laws to be absolutely void. An officer
to be appointed in each State, to have a nega-
tive on all State laws. All the militia, and the
appointments of officers, to be under the national government. I confess that this plan
and that from Virginia are very remote from
the idea of the people. Perhaps the Jersey
plan is nearest their expectation. But the
people are gradually ripening in their opinions
of government; they begin to be tired of an

excess of democracy; and what even is the Virginia plan, but "pork still, with a little change of sauce." — *Speeches in the Federal Convention*, as reported by Yates, June 18, 1787. Vol. I, pp. 381–384.

LENGTH OF PRESIDENTIAL TERM

Duration in office has been mentioned as the second requisite to the energy of the Executive authority. This has relation to two objects: to the personal firmness of the executive magistrate, in the employment of his constitutional powers; and to the stability of the system of administration which may have been adopted under his auspices. With regard to the first, it must be evident, that the longer the duration in office, the greater will be the probability of obtaining so important an advantage. It is a general principle of human nature, that a man will be interested in whatever he possesses in proportion to the firmness or precariousness of the tenure by which he holds it; will be less attached to what he holds by a momentary or uncertain title, than to what he enjoys by a durable or certain title; and, of course, will be willing to risk more for the sake of the one, than for the sake of the other. This remark is not less applicable to a political privilege, or honor, or trust, than to any article of ordinary property. The inference from it is, that a man acting in the capacity of chief magistrate, under a consciousness that in a very short time he *must* lay down his office, will be apt to feel himself too little interested in it to hazard any material censure or perplexity, from the independent exertion of his powers, or from encountering the ill-humors, however transient, which may happen to prevail, either in a considerable part of the society itself, or even in a predominant faction of the legislative body. If the case should only be, that if he should be desirous of being continued, his wishes, conspiring with his fears, would tend still more powerfully to corrupt his integrity, or debase his fortitude. In either case, feebleness and irresolution must be the characteristics of the station. — *The Federalist.* Vol. IX, pp. 445-446.

It may be asked, how the shortness of the duration in office can affect the independence of the Executive on the legislature, unless the one were possessed of the power of appointing or displacing the other. One answer to this enquiry may be drawn from the principle already remarked — that is, from the slender interest a man is apt to take in a short-lived advantage, and the little inducement it affords him to expose himself, on account of it, to any inconvenience or hazard. Another answer, perhaps more obvious, though not more conclusive, will result from the consideration of the influence of the legislative body over the people; which might be employed to prevent the reelection of a man who, by an upright resistance to any sinister project of that body, should have made himself obnoxious to its resentment.

It may be asked also, whether a duration of four years would answer the end proposed; and if it would not, whether a less period, which would at least be recommended by greater security against ambitious designs, would not, for that reason, be preferable to a longer period, which was, at the same time, too short for the purpose of inspiring the desired firmness and independence of the magistrate.

It cannot be affirmed, that a duration of four years, or any other limited duration, would completely answer the end proposed; but it would contribute towards it in a degree which would have a material influence upon

the spirit and character of the government.
Between the commencement and termination
of such a period, there would always be a considerable interval, in which the prospect of
annihilation would be sufficiently remote, not
to have an improper effect upon the conduct of
a man indued with a tolerable portion of fortitude; and in which he might reasonably
promise himself, that there would be time
enough before it arrived, to make the community sensible of the propriety of the measures
he might incline to pursue. Though it be
probable that, as he approached the moment
when the public were, by a new election, to
signify their sense of his conduct, his confidence,
and with it his firmness, would decline; yet
both the one and the other would derive support from the opportunities which his previous
continuance in the station had afforded him,
of establishing himself in the esteem and good-
will of his constituents. He might, then, hazard
with safety, in proportion to the proofs he had
given of his wisdom and integrity, and to the
title he had acquired to the respect and attachment of his fellow-citizens. — *The Federalist.*
Vol. IX, pp. 448–449.

With a positive duration of considerable extent, I connect the circumstance of reeligibility. The first is necessary to give to the officer himself the inclination and the resolution to act his part well, and to the community time and leisure to observe the tendency of his measures, and thence to form an experimental estimate of their merits. The last is necessary to enable the people, when they see reason to approve of his conduct, to continue him in his station, in order to prolong the utility of his talents and virtues, and to secure to the government the advantage of permanency in a wise system of administration.

Nothing appears more plausible at first sight, nor more illfounded upon close inspection, than a scheme which in relation to the present point has had some respectable advocates, — I mean that of continuing the chief magistrate in office for a certain time, and then excluding him from it, either for a limited period or forever after. This exclusion, whether temporary or perpetual, would have nearly the same effects, and these effects would be for the most part rather pernicious than salutary.

One ill effect of the exclusion would be a diminution of the inducements to good behavior.

HAMILTONIAN PRINCIPLES

There are few men who would not feel much less zeal in the discharge of duty, when they were conscious that the advantages of the station with which it was connected must be relinquished at a determinate period, than when they were permitted to entertain a hope of *obtaining*, by *meriting*, a continuance of them. — *The Federalist.* Vol. IX, pp. 451–452.

Another ill effect of the exclusion would be the temptation to sordid views, to peculation, and, in some instances, to usurpation. An avaricious man, who might happen to fill the office, looking forward to a time when he must at all events yield up the emoluments he enjoyed, would feel a propensity, not easy to be resisted by such a man, to make the best use of the opportunity he enjoyed while it lasted, and might not scruple to have recourse to the most corrupt expedients to make the harvest as abundant as it was transitory; though the same man, probably, with a different prospect before him, might content himself with the regular perquisites of his situation, and might even be unwilling to risk the consequences of an abuse of his opportunities. His avarice might be a guard upon his avarice. — *The Federalist.* Vol. IX, p. 452.

An ambitious man, too, when he found himself seated on the summit of his country's
honors, when he looked forward at the time at
which he must descend from the exalted emi-
nence for ever, and reflected that no exertion
of merit on his part could save him from the
unwelcome reverse; such a man, in such a
situation, would be much more violently
tempted to embrace a favorable conjuncture
for attempting the prolongation of his power,
at every personal hazard, than if he had the
probability of answering the same end by doing
his duty.

Would it promote the peace of the community, or the stability of the government to
have half a dozen men who had had credit
enough to be raised to the seat of the supreme
magistracy, wandering among the people like
discontented ghosts, and sighing for a place
which they were destined never more to possess ?

A third ill effect of the exclusion would be,
the depriving the community of the advantage
of the experience gained by the chief magistrate
in the exercise of his office. That experience is
the parent of wisdom, is an adage the truth of
which is recognized by the wisest as well as the
simplest of mankind. What more desirable or

more essential than this quality in the governors of nations? Where more desirable or more essential than in the first magistrate of a nation? Can it be wise to put this desirable and essential quality under the ban of the Constitution, and to declare that the moment it is acquired, its possessor shall be compelled to abandon the station in which it was acquired, and to which it is adapted? This, nevertheless, is the precise import of all those regulations which exclude men from serving their country, by the choice of their fellow-citizens, after they have by a course of service fitted themselves for doing it with a greater degree of utility.

A fourth ill effect of the exclusion would be the banishing men from stations in which, in certain emergencies of the state, their presence might be of the greatest moment to the public interest or safety. There is no nation which has not, at one period or another experienced an absolute necessity of the services of particular men in particular situations; perhaps it would not be too strong to say, to the preservation of its political existence. How unwise, therefore, must be every such self-denying ordinance as serves to prohibit a nation from making use of its own citizens in the manner

best suited to its exigencies and circumstances!
— *The Federalist.*   Vol. IX, pp. 453-454.

A fifth ill effect of the exclusion would be,
that it would operate as a constitutional inter-
diction of stability in the administration.   By
necessitating a change of men, in the first office
of the nation, it would necessitate a mutability
of measures.   It is not generally to be expected,
that men will vary and measures remain uniform.   The contrary is the usual course of
things. — *The Federalist.*   Vol. IX, p. 454.

What are the advantages promised to coun-
terbalance these disadvantages?   They are
represented to be: 1st, greater independence
in the magistrate; 2d, greater security to the
people.   Unless the exclusion be perpetual,
there will be no pretence to infer the first advantage.   But even in that case, may he have
no object beyond his present station, to which
he may sacrifice his independence?   May he
have no connections, no friends, for whom he
may sacrifice it?   May he not be less willing,
by a firm conduct, to make personal enemies,
when he acts under the impression that a time
is fast approaching, on the arrival of which he

not only *may*, but *must*, be exposed to their resentments, upon an equal, perhaps upon an inferior, footing? Is it not an easy point to determine whether his independence would be most promoted or impaired by such an arrangement.

As to the second supposed advantage, there is still greater reason to entertain doubts concerning it. If the exclusion were to be perpetual, a man of irregular ambition, of whom alone there could be reason in any case to entertain apprehension, would, with infinite reluctance, yield to the necessity of taking his leave forever of a post in which his passion for power and preeminence had acquired the force of habit. And if he had been fortunate or adroit enough to conciliate the good-will of the people, he might induce them to consider as a very odious and unjustifiable restraint upon themselves, a provision which was calculated to debar them of the right of giving a fresh proof of their attachment to a favorite. — *The Federalist.* Vol. IX, pp. 454–455.

The Executive and the Treaty Power

However proper or safe it may be in governments where the executive magistrate is an hereditary monarch, to commit to him the entire power of making treaties, it would be utterly unsafe and improper to intrust that power to an elective magistrate of four years' duration. It has been remarked, upon another occasion, and the remark is unquestionably just, that an hereditary monarch, though often the oppressor of his people, has personally too much stake in the government to be in any material danger of being corrupted by foreign powers. But a man raised from the station of a private citizen to the rank of chief magistrate, possessed of a moderate or slender fortune, and looking forward to a period not very remote when he may probably be obliged to return to the station from which he was taken, might sometimes be under temptations to sacrifice his duty to his interest, which it would require superlative virtue to withstand. An avaricious man might be tempted to betray the interests of the state to the acquisition of wealth. An ambitious man might make his own aggrandizement, by the aid of a foreign power, the price of his treachery to his constituents. The history of human conduct does not warrant that exalted opinion of human virtue which would make it wise in a nation to commit interests of so delicate and momentous a kind, as those which concern its intercourse with the rest of the world, to the sole disposal of a magistrate created and circumstanced as would be a President of the United States.

To have intrusted the power of making treaties to the Senate alone, would have been to relinquish the benefits of the constitutional agency of the President in the conduct of foreign negotiations. It is true that the Senate would, in that case, have the option of employing him in this capacity, but they would also have the option of letting it alone, and pique or cabal might induce the latter rather than the former. Besides this, the ministerial servant of the Senate could not be expected to enjoy the confidence and respect of foreign powers in the same degree with the constitutional representatives of the nation, and, of course, would not be able to act with an equal degree of weight or efficacy. While the Union would, from this cause, lose a considerable advantage in the management of its external concerns, the people would lose the additional security which would result from the coöperation of the Executive. Though it would be imprudent to confide in him solely so important a trust, yet it cannot be doubted that his participation would materially add to the safety of the society. It must indeed be clear to a demonstration that the joint possession of the power in question, by the President and Senate, would afford a greater prospect of security, than the separate possession of it by either of them. And whoever has maturely weighed the circumstances which must concur in the appointment of a President, will be satisfied that the office will always bid fair to be filled by men of such characters as to render their concurrence in the formation of treaties peculiarly desirable, as well on the score of wisdom, as on that of integrity.

The remarks made in a former number, which have been alluded to in another part of this paper, will apply with conclusive force against the admission of the House of Representatives to a share in the formation of treaties. The fluctuating and, taking its future increase into the account, the multitudinous composition of that body, forbid us to expect in it those qualities which are essential to the proper execution of such a trust. Accurate and comprehensive knowledge of foreign politics; a steady and systematic adherence to the same views; a nice and uniform sensibility to national character; decision, *secrecy*, and despatch, are incompatible with the genius of a body so variable and so numerous. — *The Federalist.* Vol. IX, pp. 467–469.

The legislative department is not the *organ* of intercourse between the United States and foreign nations. It is charged neither with *making* nor *interpreting* treaties. It is therefore not naturally that member of the government which is to pronounce on the existing condition of the nation with regard to foreign powers, or to admonish the citizens of their obligations and duties in consequence; still less is it charged with enforcing the observances of those obligations and duties. . . .

The province of [the judiciary] department is to decide the litigation in particular cases. It is indeed charged with the interpretations of treaties, but it exercises this function only where contending parties bring before it a specific controversy. It has no concern with pronouncing upon the external political relations of treaties between government and government. This position is too plain to need being insisted upon.

It must, then, of necessity belong to the

executive department to exercise the function in question, when a proper case for it occurs.

It appears to be connected with that department in various capacities: — As the *organ* of intercourse between the nation and foreign nations; as the *interpreter* of the national treaties, in those cases in which the judiciary is not competent — that is, between government and government; as the *power* which is charged with the execution of the laws, of which treaties form a part; as that which is charged with the command and disposition of the public force. — "*Pacificus*," 1793.   Vol. IV, pp. 139–140.

THE LEGISLATURE

THE LEGISLATURE

Legislative Powers

THE fundamental defect [of the Continental Congress before the adoption of the constitution] is a want of power in Congress. It is hardly worth while to show in what this consists, as it seems to be universally acknowledged; or to point out how it has happened, as the only question is how to remedy it. It may, however, be said, that it has originated from three causes: an excess of the spirit of liberty, which has made the particular States show a jealousy of all power not in their own hands, — and this jealousy has led them to exercise a right of judging in the last resort of the measures recommended by Congress, and of acting according to their own opinions of their propriety, or necessity; a diffidence, in Congress, of their own powers, by which they have been timid and indecisive in their resolutions, constantly making concessions to the States, till they have scarcely left themselves the shadow of power; a want of sufficient means at their disposal to answer the public exigencies, and of vigor to draw forth those means, which have occasioned them to depend on the States, individually to fulfill their engagements with the army, — the consequence of which has been to ruin their influence and credit with the army, to establish its dependence on each State separately, rather than *on them* — that is, rather than on the whole collectively.

It may be pleaded that Congress had never any definite powers granted them, and of course could exercise none, could do nothing more than recommend. The manner in which Congress was appointed would warrant, and the public good required that they should have considered themselves as vested with full power *to preserve the republic from harm*. They have done many of the highest acts of sovereignty, which were always cheerfully submitted to: The declaration of independence, the declaration of war, the levying of an army, creating a navy, emitting money, making alliances with foreign powers, appointing a dictator, etc. All these implications of a complete sovereignty were never disputed, and ought to have been a standard for the whole conduct of administration. Undefined powers are discretionary powers, limited only by the object for which they were given; in the present case the independence and freedom of America. — *Letter to James Duane*, September 3, 1780. Vol. I, pp. 203–205.

REPRESENTATION IN THE LEGISLATURE

Hence it appears that such "of the people as have no vote in the choice of representatives, and therefore are governed by laws to which they have not consented, either by themselves or by their representatives," are only those "persons who are *in so mean a situation* that they are esteemed to have *no will* of their own." Every *free agent*, every free man, possessing a freehold of forty shillings per annum, is, by the British constitution, entitled to a vote in the election of those who are invested with the disposal of his life, his liberty, and property.

It is therefore evident, to a demonstration, that unless a *free agent* in America be permitted to enjoy the same privilege, we are entirely stripped of the benefits of the constitution, and precipitated into an abyss of slavery. For we are deprived of that immunity which is the grand pillar and support of freedom. And this cannot be done without a direct violation of the constitution, which decrees to every *free agent* a share in the legislature.

It deserves to be remarked here, that those very persons in Great Britain who are *in so mean a situation* as to be excluded from a part in the elections, are in more eligible circumstances than they would be in who have every necessary qualification.

They compose a part of that society to whose government they are subject. They are nourished and maintained by it, and partake in every other emolument for which they are qualified. They have, no doubt, most of them, relations and connections among those who are privileged to vote and by that means are not entirely without influence in the appointment of their rulers. They are not governed by laws made expressly and exclusively for them, but by the general laws of their country, equally obligatory on the legal electors and on the law-makers themselves. So that they have nearly the same security against oppression which the body of the people have.

To this we may add, that they are only under a conditional prohibition, which industry and good fortune may remove. They may, one day, accumulate a sufficient property to enable them to emerge out of their present state. Or, should they die in it, their situation is not entailed upon their posterity by a fixed and irremediable doom. They, agreeably to the ordinary vicissitudes of human affairs, may acquire what their parents were deficient in. — *The Farmer Refuted*, 1775. Vol. I, pp. 86–87.

THE BASIS OF REPRESENTATION

The idea of an actual representation of all classes of the people, by persons of each class, is altogether visionary. Unless it were expressly provided in the Constitution, that each different occupation should send one or more members, the thing would never take place in practice. Mechanics and manufacturers will always be inclined, with few exceptions, to give their votes to merchants, in preference to persons of their own professions or trades. Those discerning citizens are well aware that the mechanic and manufacturing arts furnish the materials of mercantile enterprise and industry. Many of them, indeed, are immediately connected with the operations of commerce. They know that the merchant is their natural patron and friend; and they are aware, that however great the confidence they may justly feel in their own good sense, their interests can be more effectually promoted by the merchant than by themselves. They are sensible that their habits in life have not been such as to give them those acquired endowments, without which, in a deliberative assembly, the greatest natural abilities are for the most part useless; and that the influence and weight, and superior acquirements of the merchants render them more equal to a contest with any spirit which might happen to diffuse itself into the public councils, unfriendly to the manufacturing and trading interests. These considerations, and many others that might be mentioned, prove, and experience confirms it, that artisans and manufacturers will commonly be disposed to bestow their votes upon merchants as the natural representatives of all these classes of the community.

With regard to the learned professions, little need be observed; they truly form no distinct interest in society, and according to their situation and talents, will be indiscriminately the objects of the confidence and choice of each other, and of other parts of the community.

Nothing remains but the landed interest; and this, in a political view, and particularly in relation to taxes, I take to be perfectly united, from the wealthiest landlord down to the poorest tenant. No tax can be laid on land which will not affect the proprietor of millions of acres as well as the proprietor of a single acre. Every landholder will therefore have a common interest to keep the taxes on land as low as possible; and common interest may always be reckoned upon as the surest bond of sympathy. But if we even could suppose a distinction of interest between the opulent landholder and the middling farmer, what reason is there to conclude, that the first would stand a better chance of being deputed to the national legislature than the last? If we take fact as our guide, and look into our own senate and assembly [New York], we shall find that moderate proprietors of land prevail in both; nor is this less the case in the senate, which consists of a smaller number, than in the assembly, which is composed of a greater number. Where the qualifications of the electors are the same, whether they have to choose a small or large number, their votes will fall upon those in whom they have the most confidence; whether these happen to be men of large fortunes, or of moderate property, or of no property at all.

HAMILTONIAN PRINCIPLES

It is said to be necessary, that all classes of citizens should have some of their own number in the representative body, in order that their feelings and interests may be the better understood and attended to. But we have seen that this will never happen under any arrangement that leaves the votes of the people free. Where this is the case, the representative body, with too few exceptions to have any influence on the spirit of government, will be composed of landholders, merchants, and men of the learned professions. But where is the danger that the interests and feelings of the different classes of citizens will not be understood or attended to by these three descriptions of men? Will not the landholder know and feel whatever will promote or injure the interest of landed property? And will he not, from his own interest in that species of property, be sufficiently prone to resist every attempt to prejudice or encumber it? Will not the merchant understand and be disposed to cultivate, as far as may be proper, the interests of the mechanic and manufacturing arts, to which his commerce is so nearly allied? Will not the man of the learned profession, who will feel a neutrality to the rivalships between the different branches of industry, be likely to prove an impartial arbiter between them, ready to promote either, so far as it shall appear to him conducive to the general interests of the society?

If we take into account the momentary humors of dispositions which may happen to prevail in particular parts of the society, and to which a wise administration will never be inattentive, is the man whose situation leads to extensive inquiry and information less likely to be a competent judge of their nature, extent, and foundation than one whose observation does not travel beyond the circle of his neighbors and acquaintances? Is it not natural that a man who is a candidate for the favor of the people, and who is dependent on the suffrages of his fellow-citizens for the continuance of his public honors, should take care to inform himself of their dispositions and inclinations, and should be willing to allow them their proper degree of influence upon his conduct? This dependence, and the necessity of being bound himself, and his posterity, by the laws to which he gives his assent, are the true, and they are the strong chords of sympathy between the representative and the constituent. — *The Federalist.* Vol. IX, pp. 204–206.

HAMILTONIAN PRINCIPLES

Term of Legislative Service

No man can be a competent legislator who does not add to an upright intention and a sound judgment a certain degree of knowledge of the subjects on which he is to legislate. A part of this knowledge may be acquired by means of information which lie within in the compass of men on private as well as public stations. Another part can only be attained, or at least thoroughly attained, by actual experience in the station which requires the use of it. The period of service, ought, therefore, in all such cases, to bear some proportion to the extent of practical knowledge requisite to the due performance of the service. The period of legislative service established in most of the States for the more numerous branch is, as we have seen, one year. The question then may be put into this simple form: does the period of two years bear no greater proportion to the knowledge requisite for federal legislation than one year does to the knowledge requisite for State legislation? The very statement of the question, in this form, suggests the answer that ought to be given to it. — *The Federalist*. Vol. IX, pp. 335–336.

HAMILTONIAN PRINCIPLES

The Legislature and the People

The *third* charge against the House of Representatives is, that it will be taken from that class of citizens which will have the least sympathy with the mass of the people, and be most likely to aim at an ambitious sacrifice of the many to the aggrandizement of the few.

Of all the objections which have been framed against the federal Constitution, this is perhaps the most extraordinary. Whilst the objection itself is levelled against a pretended oligarchy, the principle of it strikes at the very root of republican government.

The aim of every political constitution is, or ought to be, first to obtain for rulers men who possess most wisdom to discern, and most virtue to pursue, the common good of the society; and in the next place, to take the most effectual precautions for keeping them virtuous whilst they continue to hold the public trust. The elective mode of obtaining rulers is the characteristic policy of republican government. The means relied on in this form of government for preventing their degeneracy are numerous and various. The most effectual one, is such a limitation of the term of appointments as will maintain a proper responsibility to the people. . . .

Who are to be the electors of the federal representatives? Not the rich, more than the poor; not the learned, more than the ignorant; not the haughty heirs of distinguished names, more than the humble sons of obscurity and unpropitious fortune. The electors are to be the great body of the people of the United States. They are to be the same who exercise the right in every State of electing the corresponding branch of the legislature of the State.

Who are to be the subjects of popular choice? Every citizen whose merit may recommend him to the esteem and confidence of his country. No qualification of wealth, of birth, of religious faith, or of civil profession is permitted to fetter the judgment or disappoint the inclination of the people. — *The Federalist*. Vol. IX, pp. 355-356.

SIZE OF LEGISLATIVE BODIES

In all legislative assemblies the greater the number composing them may be, the fewer will be the men who will in fact direct their proceedings. In the first place, the more numerous an assembly may be, of whatever characters composed, the greater is known to be the ascendancy of passion over reason. In the next place, the larger the number, the greater will be the proportion of members of limited information and of weak capacities. Now, it is precisely on characters of this description that the eloquence and address of the few are known to act with all their force. In the ancient republics, where the whole body of the people assembled in person, a single orator, or an artful statesman, was generally seen to rule with as complete a sway as if a sceptre had been placed in his single hand. On the same principle, the more multitudinous a representative assembly may be rendered, the more it will partake of the infirmities incident to collective meetings of the people. Ignorance will be the dupe of cunning, and passion the slave of sophistry and declamation. The people can never err more than in supposing that by multiplying their representatives beyond a certain limit, they strengthen the barrier against the government of a few. Experience will forever admonish them that, on the contrary, *after securing a sufficient number for the purposes of local information, and of diffusive sympathy with the whole society,* they will counteract their own views by every addition to their representatives. The countenance of the government may become more democratic, but the soul that animates it will be more oligarchic. The machine will be enlarged, but the fewer, and often the more secret, will be the springs by which its motions are directed.

As connected with the objection against the number of representatives, may properly be here noticed, that which has been suggested against the number made competent for legislative business. It has been said that more than a majority ought to have been required for a quorum; and in particular cases, if not in all, more than a majority of a quorum for a decision. That some advantages might have resulted from such a precaution, cannot be denied. It might have been an additional shield to some particular interests, and another obstacle to hasty and partial measures. But these considerations are outweighed by the inconveniences in the opposite scale. In all cases where justice or the general good might require new laws to be passed, or active measures to be pursued, the fundamental principle of free government would be reversed. It would be no longer the majority that would rule: the power would be transferred to the minority. Were the defensive privilege limited to particular cases, an interested minority might take advantage of it to screen themselves from equitable sacrifices to the general weal, or, in particular emergencies, to extort unreasonable indulgences. Lastly, it would facilitate and foster the baneful practice of secessions; a practice which has shown itself even in States where a majority only is required; a practice subversive of all the principles of order and regular government; a practice which leads more directly to public convulsions, and the ruin of popular governments, than any other which has yet been displayed among us. — *The Federalist*. Vol. IX, pp. 367–368.

FREQUENCY OF ELECTION

The mutability in the public councils arising from a rapid succession of new members, however qualified they may be, points out, in the strongest manner, the necessity of some stable institution in the government. Every new election in the States is found to change one half of the representatives. From this change of men must proceed a change of opinions; and from a change of opinions, a change of measures. But a continual change even of good measures is inconsistent with every rule of prudence and every prospect of success. The remark is verified in private life, and becomes more just, as well as more important, in national transactions. — *The Federalist.* Vol. IX, p. 389.

As it is essential to liberty that the government in general should have a common interest with the people, so it is particularly essential that the [legislative] branch of it . . . should have an immediate dependence on, and an intimate sympathy with, the people. Frequent elections are unquestionably the only policy by which this dependence and sympathy can be effectually secured. But what particular degree of frequency may be absolutely necessary for the purpose, does not appear to be susceptible of any precise calculation, and must depend on a variety of circumstances with which it may be connected. Let us consult experience, the guide that ought always to be followed whenever it can be found. — *The Federalist.* Vol. IX, p. 329.

THE JUDICIARY

THE JUDICIARY

THE complete independence of the courts of justice is peculiarly essential in a limited Constitution. By a limited Constitution, I understand one which contains certain specified exceptions to the legislative authority; such, for instance, as that it shall pass no bills of attainder, no *ex-post-facto* laws, and the like. Limitations of this kind can be preserved in practice no other way than through the medium of courts of justice, whose duty it must be to declare all acts contrary to the manifest tenor of the Constitution void. Without this, all the reservations of particular rights or privileges would amount to nothing.

Some perplexity respecting the rights of the courts to pronounce legislative acts void, because contrary to the Constitution, has arisen from an imagination that the doctrine would imply a superiority of the judiciary to the legislative power. It is urged that the authority which can declare the acts of another void, must necessarily be superior to the one whose acts may be declared void. As this doctrine is of great importance in all the American constitutions, a brief discussion of the ground on which it rests cannot be unacceptable.

There is no position which depends on clearer principles, than that every act of a delegated authority, contrary to the tenor of the commission under which it is exercised, is void. No legislative act, therefore, contrary to the Constitution, can be valid. To deny this, would be to affirm, that the deputy is greater than his principal; that the servant is above his master; that the representatives of the people are superior to the people themselves; that men acting by virtue of powers, may do not only what their powers authorize, but what they forbid.

If it be said that the legislative body are themselves the constitutional judges of their own powers, and that the construction they put upon them is conclusive upon the other departments, it may be answered, that this cannot be the natural presumption, where it is not to be collected from any particular provisions in the Constitution. It is not otherwise to be supposed, that the Constitution could intend to enable the representatives of the people to substitute their *will* to that of their constituents. It is far more rational to suppose, that the courts were designed to be an intermediate body between the people and the legislature, in order, among other things, to keep the latter within the limits assigned to their authority. The interpretation of the laws is the proper and peculiar province of the courts. A constitution is, in fact, and must be regarded by the judges, as a fundamental law. It therefore belongs to them to ascertain its meaning, as well as the meaning of any particular act proceeding from the legislative body. If there should happen to be an irreconcilable variance between the two, that which has the superior obligation and validity ought, of course, to be preferred to the statute, the intention of the people to the intention of their agents.

Nor does this conclusion by any means suppose a superiority of the judicial to the legislative power. It only supposes that the power of the people is superior to both; and that where the will of the legislature, declared in its statutes, stands in opposition to that of the people, declared in the Constitution, the judges ought to be governed by the latter rather than the former. They ought to regulate their decisions by the fundamental laws, rather than by those which are not fundamental. — *The Federalist.* Vol. IX, pp. 484-486.

Next to permanency in office, nothing can contribute more to the independence of the judges than a fixed provision for their support. The remark made in relation to the President is equally applicable here. In the general course of human nature, *a power over a man's subsistence amounts to a power over his will.* And we can never hope to see realized in practice, the complete separation of the judicial from the legislative power, in any system which leaves the former dependent for pecuniary resources on the occasional grants of the latter. The enlightened friends to good government in every State, have seen cause to lament the want of precise and explicit precautions in the State constitutions on this head. Some of these indeed have declared that *permanent* . . . salaries should be established for the judges; but the experiment has in some instances shown that such expressions are not sufficiently definite to preclude legislative evasions. Something still more positive and unequivocal has been evinced to be requisite. The plan of the convention accordingly has provided that the judges of the United States "shall at *stated times* receive for their services a compensation which shall not be *diminished* during their continuance in office." — *The Federalist.* Vol. IX, p. 491.

It can be of no weight to say that the courts, on the pretence of a repugnancy, may substitute their own pleasure to the constitutional intentions of the legislature. This might as well happen in the case of two contradictory statutes; or it might as well happen in every adjudication upon any single statute. The courts must declare the sense of the law; and if they should be disposed to exercise *will* instead of *judgment*, the consequence would equally be the substitution of their pleasure to that of the legislative body. The observation, if it prove anything, would prove that there ought to be no judges distinct from that body.

If, then, the courts of justice are to be considered as the bulwarks of a limited Constitution against legislative encroachments, this consideration will afford a strong argument for the permanent tenure of judicial offices, since nothing will contribute so much as this to that independent spirit in the judges which must be essential to the faithful performance of so arduous a duty. — *The Federalist.* Vol. IX, p. 487.

According to the plan of the convention, all judges who may be appointed by the United States are to hold their offices *during good behavior;* which is conformable to the most approved of the State constitutions, and among the rest, to that of this State. Its propriety having been drawn into question by the adversaries of that plan, is no light symptom of the rage for objection, which disorders their imaginations and judgments. The standard of good behavior for the continuance in office of the judicial magistracy, is certainly one of the most valuable of the modern improvements in the practice of government. In a monarchy it is an excellent barrier to the despotism of the prince; in a republic it is a no less excellent barrier to the encroachments and oppressions of the representative body. And it is the best expedient which can be devised in any government, to secure a steady, upright, and impartial administration of the laws. — *The Federalist.* Vol. IX, p. 483.

HAMILTONIAN PRINCIPLES

No man can think more highly of our judges, and I may say personally so of those who now preside, than myself; but I must forget what human nature is, and how her history has taught us that permanent bodies may be so corrupted, before I can venture to assert that it cannot be. As then it may be, I do not think it safe thus to compromise our independence. For though, as individuals, the judges may be interested in the general welfare, yet, if once they enter into these views of government, their power may be converted into the engine of oppression. It is in vain to say that allowing them this exclusive right to declare the law, on what the jury has found, can work no ill; for, by this privilege, they can assume and modify the fact, so as to make the most innocent publication libellous. It is therefore not a security to say, that this exclusive power will but follow the law. It must be with the jury to decide on the intent; they must in certain cases be permitted to judge of the law, and pronounce on the combined matter of law and of fact. Passages have been adduced from Lord Mansfield's declarations to show that judges cannot be under the influence of an administration. Yet still it would be contrary to our own experience, to say that they could not. I do not think that even as to our own country it may not be. There are always motives and reasons that may be held up. It is therefore still more necessary, here, to mingle this power, than in England. The person who appoints there, is hereditary. That person cannot alone attack the judiciary; he must be united with the two Houses of Lords and of Commons, in assailing the judges. But, with us, it is the vibration of party. As one side or the other prevails, so of that class and temperament will be the judges of their nomination. Ask any man, however ignorant of principles of government, who constitute the judiciary, he will tell you the favorites of those at the head of affairs. According then to the theory of this our free government, the independence of our judges is not so well secured as in England. We have here reasons for apprehension not applicable there. — *Speech in the New York Supreme Court*, 1804. Vol. VII, pp. 341–342.

It may in the last place be observed that the supposed danger of judiciary encroachments on the legislative authority, which has been upon many occasions reiterated, is in reality a phantom. Particular misconstructions and contraventions of the will of the legislature may now and then happen; but they can never be so extensive as to amount to an inconvenience, or in any sensible degree to affect the order of the political system. This may be inferred with certainty, from the general nature of the judicial power, from the objects to which it relates, from the manner in which it is exercised, from its comparative weakness, and from its total incapacity to support its usurpations by force. And the inference is greatly fortified by the consideration of the important constitutional check which the power of instituting impeachments in one part of the legislative body, and of determining upon them in the other, would give to that body upon the members of the judicial department. This is alone a complete security. There never can be danger that the judges, by a series of deliberate usurpations on the authority of the legislature, would hazard the united resentment of the body intrusted with it, while this body was possessed of the means of punishing their presumption, by degrading them from their stations. While this ought to remove all apprehensions on the subject, it affords, at the same time, a cogent argument for constituting the Senate a court for the trial of impeachments. — *The Federalist.* Vol. IX, p. 505.

AGRICULTURE, COMMERCE, AND MANUFACTURES

AGRICULTURE, COMMERCE, AND MANUFACTURES

It may be inferred that manufacturing establishments not only occasion a positive augmentation of the produce and revenue of the society, but that they contribute essentially to rendering them greater than they could possibly be without such establishments. These circumstances are:

1. The division of labor.

2. An extension of the use of machinery.

3. Additional employment to classes of the community not ordinarily engaged in the business.

4. The promoting of emigration from foreign countries.

5. The furnishing greater scope for the diversity of talents and dispositions, which discriminate men from each other.

6. The affording a more ample and various field for enterprise.

7. The creating, in some instances, a new,

and securing, in all, a more certain and steady demand for the surplus produce of the soil.

Each of these circumstances has a considerable influence upon the total mass of industrious effort in a community; together, they add to it a degree of energy and effect which is not easily conceived. — *Report on Manufactures*, 1791. Vol. III, p. 310.

Agriculture and Manufactures

Labor employed in agriculture is, in a great measure, periodical and occasional, depending on seasons, and liable to various and long intermissions; while that occupied in many manufactures is constant and regular, extending through the year, embracing, in some instances, night as well as day. It is also probable that there are, among the cultivators of land, more examples of remissness than among artificers. The farmer, from the peculiar fertility of his land, or some other favorable circumstance, may frequently obtain a livelihood, even with a considerable degree of carelessness in the mode of cultivation; but the artisan can with difficulty effect the same object, without exerting himself pretty equally with all those who are engaged in the same pursuit. And if it may likewise be assumed as a fact, that manufactures open a wider field to exertions of ingenuity than agriculture, it would not be a strained conjecture, that the labor employed in the former, being at once more constant, more uniform, and more ingenious, than that which is employed in the latter, will be found, at the same time, more productive. — *Report on Manufactures*, 1791.   Vol. III, pp. 301–302.

To affirm that the labor of the manufacturer is unproductive, because he consumes as much of the produce of land as he adds value to the raw material which he manufactures, is not better founded than it would be to affirm that the labor of the farmer, which furnishes materials to the manufacturer, is unproductive, because he consumes an equal value of manufactured articles.   Each furnishes a certain portion of the produce of his labor to the other, and each destroys a corresponding portion of the produce of the labor of the other.   In the meantime, the maintenance of two citizens, instead of one, is going on; the State has two members instead of one; and they, together, consume twice the value of what is produced from the land. — *Report on Manufactures*, 1791. Vol. III, pp. 306–307.

Considering how fast and how much the progress of new settlements in the United States must increase the surplus produce of the soil, and weighing seriously the tendency of the system which prevails among most of the commercial nations of Europe, whatever dependence may be placed on the force of natural circumstances to counteract the effects of an artificial policy, there appear strong reasons to regard the foreign demand for that surplus as too uncertain a reliance, and to desire a substitute for it in an extensive domestic market.

To secure such a market, there is no other expedient than to promote manufacturing establishments. Manufacturers, who constitute the most numerous class, after the cultivators of land, are for that reason the principal consumers of the surplus of their labor.

This idea of an extensive domestic market for the surplus produce of the soil, is of the first consequence. It is, of all things, that which most effectually conduces to a flourishing state of agriculture. If the effect of manufactories should be to detach a portion of the hands which would otherwise be engaged in tillage, it might possibly cause a smaller quantity of lands to be under cultivation; but, by their tendency to procure a more certain demand for the surplus produce of the soil, they would, at the same time, cause the lands which were in cultivation to be better improved and more productive. . . .

It is the interest of nations to diversify the industrious pursuits of the individuals who compose them ; . . . the establishment of manufactures is calculated not only to increase the general stock of useful and productive labor, but even to improve the state of agriculture in particular, — certainly to advance the interests of those who are engaged in it. — *Report on Manufactures*, 1791.   Vol. III, p. 321.

Commerce

The prosperity of commerce is now perceived and acknowledged by all enlightened statesmen to be the most useful as well as the most productive source of national wealth, and has accordingly become a primary object of their political cares. By multiplying the means of gratification, by promoting the introduction and circulation of the precious metals, those darling objects of human avarice and enterprise, it serves to vivify and invigorate the channels of industry, and to make them flow with greater activity and copiousness. The assiduous merchant, the laborious husbandman, the active mechanic, and the industrious manufacturer, — all orders of men, look forward with eager expectation and growing alacrity to this pleasing reward of their toils. The often-agitated question between agriculture and commerce has, from indubitable experience, received a decision which has silenced the rivalship that once subsisted between them, and has proved, to the satisfaction of their friends, that their interests are intimately blended and interwoven. It has been found in various countries that, in proportion as commerce has flourished, land has risen in value. And how could it have happened otherwise? Could that which procures a freer vent for the products of the earth, which furnishes new incitements to the cultivation of land, which is the most powerful instrument in increasing the quantity of money in a state — could that, in fine, which is the faithful handmaid of labor and industry, in every shape, fail to augment that article, which is the prolific parent of far the greatest part of the objects upon which they are exerted? — *The Federalist*, Vol. IX, pp. 67–68.

THE NATIONAL DEBT

THE NATIONAL DEBT

A NATIONAL debt, if it is not excessive, will be to us a national blessing. It will be a powerful cement of our Union. It will also create a necessity for keeping up taxation to a degree which, without being oppressive, will be a spur to industry, remote as we are from Europe, and shall be from danger. It were otherwise to be feared our popular maxims would incline us to too great parsimony and indulgence. We labor less now than any civilized nation of Europe; and a habit of labor is as essential to the health and vigor of their minds and bodies, as it is conducive to the welfare of the state. We ought not to suffer our self-love to deceive us in a comparison on these points. — *Letter to Robert Morris*, April 30, 1781. Vol. III, p. 124.

With the *creation* of debt, should be incorporated the *means* of extinguishment; which means are twofold: 1. *The establishing, at the time of contracting a debt, funds for the reimbursement of the principal*, as well as for the payment of interest within a determinate period. 2. The *making it a part of the contract*, that the fund, so established, shall be inviolably applied to the object.

It is believed that it would be happy for the United States, if Congress would adopt this principle as a rule in all future loans — never to be departed from; and a good evidence of this determination will be, to apply it to the past. — *Report on the Public Credit*, 1795. Vol. III, pp. 14-15.

Taxation of Government Debts

Is there a right in a government to tax its own funds?

The pretence of this right is deduced from the general right of the legislative power to make all the property of the state contributory to its own exigencies.

But this right is obviously liable to be restricted by the *engagements* of the *government;* it cannot be justly exercised in contravention of them; they must form an exception. It will not be denied, that the general right in question could, and would, be abridged by an express promise not to tax the funds. This promise, indeed, has not been given in terms, but it has been given in substance. When an individual lends money to the state, the state stipulates to repay him the principal lent, with a certain interest, or to pay a certain interest, indefinitely, till the principal is reimbursed; or it stipulates something equivalent, in another form. In our case, the stipulation is in the second form.

To tax the funds, is manifestly either to *take*, or to *keep back*, a portion of the principal or interest *stipulated to be paid*.

To do this, on whatever pretext, is *not to do what is expressly promised*; it is not to pay that precise principal, or that precise interest, which has been engaged to be paid; it is, therefore, to violate the promise given to the lender.

But is not the stipulation to the lender, a tacit reservation of the general right of the Legislature to raise contributions on the property of the state?

This cannot be supposed — because it involves two contradictory things; an *obligation to do*, and a *right not to do*. An obligation to *pay a certain sum*, and a *right to retain it in the shape of a tax*. It is against the rules, both of law and reason, to admit, by *implication*, in the construction of a contract, a principle which goes in destruction of it.

The government, by such a construction, would be made to say to the lender: "I want a sum of money, for a national purpose, which all the citizens ought to contribute proportionably, but it will be more convenient to them, and to me, to borrow the money of you. If you will lend it, I promise you faithfully, to allow you a *certain rate* of interest, while I keep the money, and to *reimburse the principal* within a determinate period, *except so much of the* one and the other as I may think fit to *withhold, in the shape of a tax.*"

Is such a construction either natural or rational? Does it not, in fact, nullify the promise by the reservation of a right not to perform it? — *Report on the Public Credit*, 1795. Vol. III, pp. 24–26.

Public debt can scarcely, in legal phrase, be defined either as *property* in possession or action. It is evidently not the first, till it is reduced to possession by payment. To be the second, would suppose a *legal power* to *compel* payment by *suit*. Does such a power exist? The true definition of public debt is *a property subsisting in the faith of the government. Its essence is promise.* Its definite value depends upon the reliance that the promise will be definitely fulfilled. Can the government rightfully tax its promise? Can it put its faith under contribution? Where or *what* is the value of the debt, if such a right exists? . . .

When a government enters into contract with an individual, it deposes as to the matter of the contract its constitutional authority, and exchanges the character of legislator for that of a moral agent, with the same rights and obligations as an individual. Its promises may be justly considered as excepted out of its *power to legislate,* unless in aid of them. It is, in theory, impossible to reconcile the two ideas of *a promise which obliges* with a *power to make a law which can vary the effect of it.* This is the great principle that governs the question, and abridges the general right of the government to lay taxes, excepting out of it a species of property which subsists only in its promise. — *Report on the Public Credit,* 1795. Vol. III, pp. 27, 29.

THE TARIFF

THE TARIFF

If the system of perfect liberty to industry and commerce were the prevailing system of nations, the arguments which dissuade a country, in the predicament of the United States, from the zealous pursuit of manufactures, would doubtless have great force. It will not be affirmed that they might not be permitted, with few exceptions, to serve as a rule of national conduct. In such a state of things, each country would have the full benefit of its peculiar advantages to compensate for its deficiencies or disadvantages. . . .

But the system which has been mentioned is far from characterizing the general policy of nations. The prevalent one has been regulated by an opposite spirit. The consequence of it is, that the United States are, to a certain extent, in the situation of a country precluded from foreign commerce. They can, indeed, without difficulty, obtain from abroad the manufactured supplies of which they are in want; but they experience numerous and very injurious impediments to the emission and vent of their own commodities. Nor is this the case in reference to a single foreign nation only. The regulations of several countries, with which we have the most extensive intercourse, throw serious obstructions in the way of the principal staples of the United States.

In such a position of things, the United States cannot exchange with Europe on equal terms; and the want of reciprocity would render them the victim of a system which should induce them to confine their views to agriculture, and refrain from manufactures. A constant and increasing necessity, on their part, for the commodities of Europe, and only a partial and occasional demand for their own, in return, could not but expose them to a state of impoverishment, compared with the opulence to which their political and natural advantages authorize them to aspire. — *Report on Manufactures*, 1791. Vol. III, pp. 323-324.

Whatever room there may be for an expectation that the industry of a people, under the direction of private interest, will, upon equal terms, find out the most beneficial employment for itself, there is none for a reliance that it

will struggle against the force of unequal terms,
or will, of itself, surmount all the adventitious
barriers to a successful competition which may
have been erected, either by the advantages
naturally acquired from practice and previous
possession of the ground, or by those which may
have sprung from positive regulations and an
artificial policy. This general reflection might
alone suffice as an answer to the objection under
examination, exclusively of the weighty considerations which have been particularly urged.
— *Report on Manufactures*, 1791. Vol. II,
pp. 329–330.

Duties of this nature [protective] evidently
amount to a virtual bounty on the domestic
fabrics; since, by enhancing the charges on
foreign articles, they enable the national manufacturers to undersell all their foreign competi-
tors. The propriety of this species of encouragement need not be dwelt upon, as it is not
only a clear result from the numerous topics
which have been suggested, but is sanctioned
by the laws of the United States, in a variety
of instances; it has the additional recommendation of being a resource of revenue. Indeed,
all the duties imposed on imported articles,

though with an exclusive view to revenue, have the effect, in contemplation, and, except where they fall on raw materials, wear a beneficent aspect toward the manufacturers of the country.

[The prohibition of foreign articles or placing import duties equivalent to prohibition] is another and an efficacious means of encouraging national manufactures; but, in general, it is only fit to be employed when a manufacture has made such progress, and is in so many hands, as to insure a due competition, and an adequate supply on reasonable terms. . . . Considering a monopoly of the domestic market to its own manufacturers as the reigning policy of manufacturing nations, a similar policy on the part of the United States, in every proper instance, is dictated, it might almost be said, by the principles of distributive justice; certainly, by the duty of endeavoring to secure to their own citizens a reciprocity of advantages. — *Report on Manufactures*, 1791. Vol. II, p. 365.

BOUNTIES

It cannot escape notice, that a duty upon the importation of an article can no otherwise aid the domestic production of it, than by giving the latter greater advantages in the home market. It can have no influence upon the advantageous sale of the article produced in foreign markets — no tendency, therefore, to promote its exportation.

The true way to conciliate these two interests is to lay a duty on foreign manufactures of the material, the growth of which is desired to be encouraged, and to apply the produce of that duty, by way of bounty, either upon the production of the material itself, or upon its manufacture at home or upon both. In this disposition of the thing, the manufacturer commences his enterprise under every advantage which is attainable, as to quantity or price of the raw material; and the farmer, if the bounty be immediately to him, is enabled by it to enter into a successful competition with the foreign material. . . .

Except the simple and ordinary kinds of household manufacture, or those for which there are very commanding local advantages, pecuniary bounties are, in most cases, indispensable to the introduction of a new branch. A stimulus and a support, not less powerful and direct, is, generally speaking, essential to the overcoming of the obstacles which arise from the competitions of superior skill and maturity elsewhere. Bounties are especially essential in regard to articles upon which those foreigners, who have been accustomed to supply a country, are in the practice of granting them.

The continuance of bounties on manufactures long established must almost always be of questionable policy; because a presumption would arise, in every such case, that there were natural and inherent impediments to success. But, in new undertakings, they are as justifiable as they are oftentimes necessary.

There is a degree of prejudice against bounties, from an appearance of giving away the public money without an immediate consideration, and from a supposition that they serve to enrich particular classes at the expense of the community.

But neither of these sources of dislike will bear a serious examination. There is no purpose to which public money can be more beneficially applied than to the acquisition of a new and useful branch of industry; no consideration more valuable than a permanent addition to the general stock of productive labor.

As to the second source of objection, it equally lies against other modes of encouragement, which are admitted to be eligible. As often as a duty upon a foreign article makes an addition to its price, it causes an extra expense to the community for the benefit of the domestic manufacturer. A bounty does no more. But it is the interest of the society, in each case, to submit to the temporary expense — which is more than compensated by an increase of industry and wealth, by an augmentation of resources and independence, and by the circumstance of eventual cheapness. — *Report on Manufactures*, 1791. Vol. III, pp. 368–370.

THE BANK

THE BANK

The National Bank

This [a national bank] I regard, in some shape or other, as an expedient essential to our safety and success. . . . There is no other that can give to government that extensive and systematic credit which the defect of our revenues makes indispensably necessary to its operations. The longer it is delayed the more difficult it becomes. . . . I am aware of all the objections that have been made to public banks; and that they are not without enlightened and respectable opponents. But all that has been said against them only tends to prove that, like all other good things, they are subject to abuse, and when abused, become pernicious. . . . The tendency of a national bank is to increase public and private credit. The former gives power to the state, for the protection of its rights and interests: and the latter facilitates and extends the operations of commerce among individuals. Industry is increased, commodities are multiplied, agriculture and manufactures flourish: and herein consists the true wealth and prosperity of a state. — *Letter to Robert Morris*, April 30, 1781. Vol. I, pp. 100–101.

MISCELLANEOUS

MISCELLANEOUS

IMMIGRATION

THE safety of a republic depends essentially
on the energy of a common national sentiment;
on a uniformity of principles and habits; on
the exemption of the citizens from foreign bias,
and prejudice; and on that love of country
which will almost invariably be found to be
closely connected with birth, education, and
family.

The opinion advanced in the Notes on Virginia is undoubtedly correct, that foreigners
will generally be apt to bring with them attach-
ments to the persons they have left behind; to
the country of their nativity, and to particular
customs and manners. They will also entertain
opinions on government congenial with those
under which they have lived; or, if they should
be led hither from a preference to ours, how extremely unlikely is it that they will bring with
them that *temperate love of liberty*, so essential
to real republicanism? There may, as to particular individuals, and at particular times, be

occasional exceptions to these remarks,[1] yet such is the general rule. The influx of foreigners must, therefore, tend to produce a heterogeneous compound; to change and corrupt the national spirit; to complicate and confound public opinion; to introduce foreign propensities. In the composition of society, the harmony of the ingredients is all-important, and whatever tends to a discordant intermixture must have an injurious tendency.

The United States have already felt the evils of incorporating a large number of foreigners into their national mass; by promoting in different classes different predilections in favor of particular foreign nations, and antipathies against others, it has served very much to divide the community and to distract our councils. It has been often likely to compromit the interests of our own country in favor of another. The permanent effect of such a policy will be, that in times of great public danger there will be always a numerous body of men, of whom there may be just grounds of distrust; the suspicion alone will weaken the strength of the nation, but their force may be actually employed in assisting an invader. —

[1] Hamilton himself was a foreign immigrant. — EDITOR

HAMILTONIAN PRINCIPLES

"Lucius Crassus," 1802. Vol. VII, pp. 241–242.

Amendments to the Constitution

As the people are the only legitimate fountain of power, and it is from them that the constitutional charter, under which the several branches of government hold their power, is derived, it seems strictly consonant to the republican theory, to recur to the same original authority, not only whenever it may be necessary to enlarge, diminish, or new-model the powers of the government, but also whenever any one of the departments may commit encroachments on the chartered authorities of the others. The several departments being perfectly coordinate by the terms of their common commission, none of them, it is evident, can pretend to an exclusive or superior right of settling the boundaries between their respective powers; and how are the encroachments of the stronger to be prevented, or the wrongs of the weaker to be redressed, without an appeal to the people themselves, who, as grantors of the commission, can alone declare its true meaning, and enforce its observance?

There is certainly great force in this reasoning,

and it must be allowed to prove that a constitutional road to the decision of the people ought
to be marked out and kept open, for certain
great and extraordinary occasions. But there
appear to be insuperable objections against the
proposed recurrence to the people, as a provision
in all cases for keeping the several departments
of power within their constitutional limits.

In the first place, the provision does not reach
the case of a combination of two of the departments against the third. If the legislative
authority, which possesses so many means of
operating on the motives of the other departments, should be able to gain to its interest
either of the others, or even one third of its
members, the remaining department could
derive no advantage from its remedial provision. I do not dwell, however, on this
objection, because it may be thought to be
rather against the modification of the principle,
than against the principle itself.

In the next place, it may be considered as an
objection inherent in the principle, that as
every appeal to the people would carry an
implication of some defect in the government,
frequent appeals would, in a great measure,
deprive the government of that veneration

which time bestows on everything, and without which perhaps the wisest and freest governments would not possess the requisite stability. If it be true that all governments rest on opinion, it is no less true that the strength of opinion in each individual, and its practical influence on his conduct, depend much on the number which he supposes to have entertained the same opinion. The reason of man, like man himself, is timid and cautious when left alone, and acquires firmness and confidence in proportion to the number with which it is associated. When the examples which fortify opinion are *ancient* as well as *numerous*, they are known to have a double effect. In a nation of philosophers, this consideration ought to be disregarded. A reverence for the laws would be sufficiently inculcated by the voice of an enlightened reason. But a nation of philosophers is as little to be expected as the philosophical race of kings wished for by Plato. And in every other nation, the most rational government will not find it a superfluous advantage to have the prejudices of the community on its side.

The danger of disturbing the public tranquillity by interesting too strongly the public passions, is a still more serious objection against

a frequent reference of constitutional questions
to the decision of the whole society. Notwithstanding the success which has attended the
revisions of our established forms of government, and which does so much honor to the
virtue and intelligence of the people of America,
it must be confessed that the experiments are
of too ticklish a nature to be unnecessarily
multiplied. We are to recollect that all the
existing constitutions were formed in the midst
of a danger which repressed the passions most
unfriendly to order and concord; of an enthu-
siastic confidence of the people in their patriotic
leaders, which stifled the ordinary diversity of
opinions on great national questions; of a
universal resentment and indignation against
the ancient government; and whilst no spirit
of party connected with the changes to be made,
or the abuses to be reformed, could mingle its
leaven in the operation. The future situations
in which we must expect to be usually placed,
do not present any equivalent security against
the danger which is apprehended.

But the greatest objection of all is, that the
decisions which would probably result from such
appeals would not answer the purpose of main-
taining the constitutional equilibrium of gov-

ernment. . . . It [such an appeal] could never be expected to turn on the true merits of the question. It would inevitably be connected with the spirit of preexisting parties, or of parties springing out of the question itself. It would be connected with persons of distinguished character and extensive influence in the community. It would be pronounced by the very men who had been agents in, or opponents of, the measures to which the decision would relate. The *passions*, therefore, not the *reason*, of the public would sit in judgment. But it is the reason alone of the public, that ought to control and regulate the government. The passions ought to be controlled and regulated by the government. — *The Federalist*. Vol. IX, pp. 314–318.

Freedom of the Press

The liberty of the press consists, in my idea, in publishing the truth, from good motives and for justifiable ends, though it reflect on the government, on magistrates, or individuals. If it be not allowed, it excludes the privilege of canvassing men, and our rulers. It is vain to say, you may canvass measures. This is impossible without the right of looking to men.

To say that measures can be discussed, and that there shall be no bearing on those who are the authors of those measures, cannot be done. The very end and reason of discussion would be destroyed. Of what consequence to show its object? Why is it to be thus demonstrated, if not to show, too, who is the author? It is essential to say, not only that the measure is bad and deleterious, but to hold up to the people who is the author, that, in this our free and elective government, he may be removed from the seat of power. If this be not done, then, in vain will the voice of the people be raised against the inroads of tyranny. For, let a party but get into power, they may go on from step to step, and, in spite of canvassing their measures, fix themselves firmly in their seats, especially as they are never to be reproached for what they have done. This abstract mode, in practice, can never be carried into effect. But if, under the qualifications I have mentioned, the power be allowed, the liberty for which I contend will operate as a salutary check. In speaking thus for the freedom of the press, I do not say there ought to be unbridled license; or that the characters of men who are good will naturally tend eternally to support

HAMILTONIAN PRINCIPLES

themselves. I do not stand here to say that no shackles are to be laid on this license. — *Speech in the New York Supreme Court*, 1804. Vol. VII, pp. 339–340.

Internal Free Trade

An unrestrained intercourse between the States themselves will advance the trade of each by an interchange of their respective productions, not only for the supply of reciprocal wants at home, but for exportation to foreign markets. The veins of commerce in every part will be replenished, and will acquire additional motion and vigor from a free circulation of the commodities of every part. Commercial enterprise will have much greater scope, from the diversity in the productions of different States. When the staple of one fails from a bad harvest or unproductive crop, it can call to its aid the staple of another. The variety, not less than the value, of products for exportation contributes to the activity of foreign commerce. It can be conducted upon much better terms with a large number of materials of a given value than with a small number of materials of the same value; arising from the competitions of trade and from the fluctuations of markets.

Particular articles may be in great demand at certain periods, and unsalable at others; but if there be a variety of articles, it can scarcely happen that they should all be at one time in the latter predicament, and on this account the operations of the merchant would be less liable to any considerable obstruction or stagnation. The speculative trader will at once perceive the force of these observations, and will acknowledge that the aggregate balance of the commerce of the United States would bid fair to be much more favorable than that of the thirteen States without union or with partial unions.

It may perhaps be replied to this, that whether the States are united or disunited, there would still be an intimate intercourse between them which would answer the same ends; but this intercourse would be fettered, interrupted, and narrowed by a multiplicity of causes. . . . A unity of commercial, as well as political interests, can only result from a unity of government. — *The Federalist*. Vol. IX, pp. 65–66.

FRANCE

The generosity of France and the magnitude of the United States have often been suggested by some of our own citizens, and we are now

[178]

reproached with it by France herself. Gratitude is due for favors received; and this virtue may exist among nations as well as among individuals; but the motive of the benefit must be solely the advantage of the party on whom it was conferred, else it ceases to be a favor. There is proof positive that France did not enter into an alliance with us in 1778 *for our advantage*, but for her own. The whole course of the investigation, as well as a positive knowledge of the fact, proves this. She resisted all of our solicitations for effectual assistance for war for three years; and rose in her demand during the campaign of 1777, when our affairs presented the most threatening aspect. Memorials were presented in August and September of that year, while General Burgoyne's army arrived in December; fearing we might be able to do the business without them, the French court began to change its tone. In January the British minister gave notice in the House of Commons that he meant to propose terms of accommodation with America. The French ministry, on the arrival of this intelligence in France, immediately pressed the conclusion of the treaty which they had resisted for three years, and proposed terms much more favorable for us than those our commissioner had offered, and they had refused three months before. The treaty was signed on the 8th of February. I perceive no generosity in all this. They did then as we have done now, and as every discerning nation will do — they regarded only their own interest and advantage, and not that of any other nation. In the interval between the declaration of independence and the alliance with France, that court sometimes ordered away our privateers, and sometimes restored their prizes. They refused to receive an ambassador or acknowledge our independence; all of which was for fear of bringing France prematurely into the war. The fact is, that the French spoke of very different terms, as the condition of their assistance before the capture of Burgoyne, from those actually agreed on afterwards. There can be no doubt that our success on that occasion, and the disposition it appeared to have produced in the British ministry, were the immediate causes of that alliance. It was certainly to interest of the French to unite with America in the war against Great Britain. They therefore acted right in doing this at last. — *"The Answer,"* 1796. Vol. V, pp. 360–361.

HAMILTONIAN PRINCIPLES

LOUISIANA

Since the question of independence, none has occurred more deeply interesting to the United States than the cession of Louisiana to France [by Spain]. . . .

The strict right to resort at once to war, if it should be deemed expedient, cannot be doubted. A manifest and great danger to the nation; the nature of the cession to France, extending to ancient limits without respect to our rights by treaty; the direct infraction of an important article of the treaty itself, in withholding the deposit of New Orleans: either of these affords justifiable cause of war, and that they would authorize immediate hostilities, is not to be questioned by the most scrupulous mind.

The whole is then a question of expediency. Two courses only present: First, to negotiate, and endeavor to purchase; and if this fails, go to war. Secondly, to seize at once on the Floridas and New Orleans, and then negotiate. A strong objection offers itself to the first. There is not the most distant probability that the ambitious and aggrandizing views of Buonaparte will commute the territory for money. . . . The attempt, therefore, to purchase . . . will certainly fail. . . . The second plan is, therefore, evidently the best. . . . If the President would adopt this course, he might yet retrieve his character, induce the best part of the community to look favorably upon his political career, exalt himself in the eyes of Europe, save the country, and secure a permanent fame. But, for this, alas! Jefferson is not destined.[1]— *"Pericles,"* 1803.   Vol. V, pp. 465-467.

War

This plan [of France to capture neutral ships] is pregnant with the worst evils, which are to be dreaded from the declared and unqualified hostility of any foreign power. If France, after being properly called upon to renounce it, shall persevere in the measure, there cannot be a question but that open war will be preferable to such a state. By whatever name treachery or pusillanimity may attempt to disguise it, 't is in fact war of the worst kind, *war on one side.* If we can be induced to submit to it longer than is necessary to ascertain that it

---

[1] He was " destined " before May 2 to sign a treaty by which he bought the immense empire peaceably for the incredibly small sum of $15,000,000. — EDITOR

cannot be averted by negotiation, we are un-
done as a people. Whether our determination
shall be to coop up our trade by embargoes, or
to permit our commerce to continue to float an
unprotected prey to French cruisers, our degra-
dation and ruin will be equally complete. The
destruction of our navigation and commerce,
the annihilation of our mercantile capital, the
dispersion and loss of our seamen — obliged to
emigrate for subsistence — the extinction of
our revenue, the fall of public credit, the stagnation of every species of industry, the general
impoverishment of our citizens, — these will be
minor evils in the dreadful catalogue. Some
years of security and exertion might repair
them. But the humiliation of the American
mind would be a lasting and a mortal disease
in our social habit. Mental debasement is the
greatest misfortune that can befall a people.
The most pernicious of conquests which a
state can experience is a conquest over that
just and elevated sense of its own rights which
inspires a due sensibility to insult and injury;
over that virtuous and generous pride of character, which prefers any peril or sacrifice to a
final submission to oppression, and which
regards national ignominy as the greatest of

national calamities. — *"The Warning,"* 1797. Vol. V, pp. 376–377.

The Navy

A further resource for influencing the conduct of European nations toward us, in this respect, would arise from the establishment of a federal navy. There can be no doubt that the continuance of the Union under an efficient government, would put it in our power, at a period not very distant, to create a navy which, if it could not vie with those of the great maritime powers, would at least be of respectable weight if thrown into the scale of either of the two contending parties. This would be more peculiarly the case in relation to operations in the West Indies. A few ships of the line, sent opportunely to the reinforcement of either side, would often be sufficient to decide the fate of a campaign. . . . A price would be set not only upon our friendship but upon our neutrality. By a steady adherence to the Union, we may hope, ere long, to become the arbiter of Europe in America, and to be able to incline the balance of European competitions in this part of the world as our interest may dictate. — *The Federalist.* Vol. IX, p. 62.

HAMILTONIAN PRINCIPLES

The Militia

I expect we shall be told that the militia of the country is its natural bulwark, and would be at all times equal to its national defence. This doctrine, in substance, had like to have lost us our independence. It cost millions to the United States that might have been saved. The facts which, from our own experience, forbid a reliance of this kind, are too recent to permit us to be the dupes of such a suggestion. The steady operations of war against a regular and disciplined army can only be successfully conducted by a force of the same kind. Considerations of economy, not less than of stability and vigor, confirm this position. The American militia, in the course of the late war, have, by their valor on numerous occasions, erected eternal monuments to their fame; but the bravest of them feel and know that the liberty of their country could not have been established by their efforts alone, however great and valuable they were. War, like most other things, is a science to be acquired and perfected by diligence, by perseverance, by time, and by practice. — *The Federalist*. Vol. IX, p. 150.

HAMILTONIAN PRINCIPLES

The right to seize and confiscate individual property, in national wars, excludes all those cases where the individual derives his title from the enemy sovereign or nation: for the right to property always implies the right to be protected and secured in the enjoyment of that property; and a nation, by the very act of permitting the citizen of a foreign country to acquire property within its territory, whether to lands, funds, or to any other thing, tacitly engages to give protection and security to that property, and to allow him as full enjoyment of it as any other proprietor — an engagement which no state of things between the two nations can justly or reasonably affect. Though politically right, that, in wars between nations, the property of private persons, which depend on the *laws of their own country*, or on *circumstances foreign to the nation with which their own is at war*, should be subject to seizure and confiscation by the enemy nation; yet it is both politically and morally wrong, that this should extend to property acquired under the faith of the government, and the laws of the enemy nation.

HAMILTONIAN PRINCIPLES

When the government enters into a contract with the citizen of a foreign country, it considers him *as an individual in a state of nature, and contracts with him as such.* It does not contract with him as *the member of another society.*

The contracts, therefore, with him cannot be affected by his political relations to that society. War, whatever right it may give over his other property, can give none over that which he derives from those contracts. The character in which they are made with him, the faith pledged to him personally, virtually exempt it.

This principle, which seems critically correct, would exempt as well the income as the capital of the property. It protects the use as effectually as the thing. What, in fact, is property, but a fiction, without the beneficial use of it? In many cases, indeed, the *income* or *annuity* is the property itself. And, although general usage may control the principle, it can only be as far as the usage clearly goes. It must not be extended by analogy.

Some of the most approved publicists, admitting the principle, qualify it with regard to the income of lands, which they say may be sequestered "to hinder the remittance of it to the enemy's country."

HAMILTONIAN PRINCIPLES

But the same authority affirms that a state of war "does not so much *as touch* the sums which it owes to the enemy. *Everywhere*, in case of a war, funds credited to the public, are exempt from confiscation and *seizure*." These expressions clearly exclude sequestration as well as confiscation.

The former no less than the latter, would be inconsistent with the declarations that a state of war does not *so much as touch* the sums which it owes to the enemy, and, that funds credited to the public are exempt from *seizure*. And, on full inquiry, it is believed that the suggestion, thus understood, is founded in fact.

Usage, then, however it may deviate in other particulars, in respect to public funds, concurs with principle in pronouncing, that they cannot rightfully be sequestrated in time of war. — *Report on the Public Credit*, 1795. Vol. III, pp. 33-35.

www.ingramcontent.com/pod-product-compliance
Lightning Source LLC
Chambersburg PA
CBHW022046050726
47591CB00002B/409